DEATH

FOUNTAINHEAD PRESS V SERIES

Edited by
Rachelle M. Smith

FOUNTAINHEAD
PRESS

MT SAN JACINTO COLLEGE
SAN JACINTO CAMPUS LIBRARY
1499 N STATE ST
SAN JACINTO, CA 92583

W9-CUD-032

Our green initiatives include:

Electronic Products
We deliver products in non-paper form whenever possible. This includes pdf downloadables, flash drives, and CDs.

Electronic Samples
We use Xample, a new electronic sampling system. Instructor samples are sent via a personalized Web page that links to pdf downloads.

FSC Certified Printers
All of our printers are certified by the Forest Service Council, which promotes environmentally and socially responsible management of the world's forests. This program allows consumer groups, individual consumers, and businesses to work together hand-in-hand to promote responsible use of the world's forests as a renewable and sustainable resource.

Recycled Paper
Most of our products are printed on a minimum of 30% post-consumer waste recycled paper.

Support of Green Causes
When we do print, we donate a portion of our revenue to green causes. Listed below are a few of the organizations that have received donations from Fountainhead Press. We welcome your feedback and suggestions for contributions, as we are always searching for worthy initiatives.
Rainforest 2 Reef
Environmental Working Group

Cover Image: © Can Stock Photo Inc. / rorem

Design by Susan Moore

Copyright © 2012 by Fountainhead Press

All rights reserved. No part of this book may be reproduced or utilized in any form or by any means, electronic or mechanical, including photocopying and recording, or by any informational storage and retrieval system without written permission from the publisher.

Books may be purchased for educational purposes.

For information, please call or write:

1-800-586-0330

Fountainhead Press
Southlake, TX 76092

Web site: www.fountainheadpress.com
E-mail: customerservice@fountainheadpress.com

First Edition

ISBN: 978-1-59871-553-8

Printed in the United States of America

INTRODUCTION TO THE FOUNTAINHEAD PRESS V SERIES

By Brooke Rollins and Lee Bauknight
Series Editors

The *Fountainhead Press V Series* is a new collection of single-topic readers that take a unique look at some of today's most pressing issues. Designed to give writing students a more nuanced introduction to public discourse—on the environment, on food, and on digital life, to name a few of the topics—the books feature writing, research, and invention prompts that can be adapted to nearly any kind of college writing class. Each *V Series* textbook focuses on a single issue and includes multi-genre and multimodal readings and assignments that move the discourse beyond the most familiar patterns of debate—patterns usually fettered by entrenched positions and often obsessed with "winning."

The ultimate goal of the series is to help writing students—who tend to hover on the periphery of public discourse—think, explore, find their voices, and skillfully compose texts in a variety of media and genres. Not only do the books help students think about compelling issues and how they might address them, they also give students the practice they need to develop their research, rhetorical, and writing skills. Together, the readings, prompts, and longer assignments show students how to add their voices to the conversations about these issues in meaningful and productive ways.

With enough readings and composing tasks to sustain an entire quarter or semester, and inexpensive enough to be used in combination with other rhetorics and readers, the *Fountainhead Press V Series* provides instructors with the flexibility to build the writing courses they want and need to teach. An instructor interested in deeply exploring environmental issues, for example, could design a semester- or quarter-long course using *Green*, the first of the *V Series* texts. At the same time, an instructor who wanted to teach discrete units on different issues could use two or more of the *V Series* books. In either case, the texts would give students ample opportunity—and a variety of ways—to engage with the issues at hand.

The *V Series* uses the term "composition" in its broadest sense. Of course, the textbooks provide students plenty of opportunities to write, but they also include assignments that take students beyond the page. Books in the series encourage students to explore other modes of communication by prompting them: to design websites, to produce videos, posters, and presentations; to conduct primary and secondary research; and to develop projects with community partners that might incorporate any number of these skills. Ultimately, we have designed the *Fountainhead Press V Series* to work for teachers and students. With their carefully chosen readings, built-in flexibility, and sound rhetorical grounding, the *V Series* books would be a dynamic and user-friendly addition to any writing class.

TABLE OF CONTENTS

INTRODUCTION: DEATH IS NEVER SPOKEN OF HERE

By Rachelle M. Smith

In the second decade of the twenty-first century, those of us fortunate enough to live in the United States and other developed nations enjoy the blessings of modern civilization. Thanks to science, technology, and good government, we live in communities that are relatively peaceful and prosperous. Modern life provides us with abundant food, good shelter from the elements, and health care that has extended our life expectancy well past that of our ancestors—or even our grandparents. It's no wonder then that death today has become something of a mystery for us, despite the fact that we will all eventually die.

Part of the mystery surrounding death is due to the fact that we, unlike previous generations, seldom witness it. In England in the 1600s, two-thirds of all children died before the age of four. Can you imagine what it must have been like to have two out of three of your brothers and sisters die in childhood? As recently as the 1950s in America, tens of thousands of children died from polio before Jonas Salk's vaccine virtually eradicated it. Today, relatively few children in the United States die from disease or malnutrition. Modern life has extended the lives of adults as well. Before modern times, if you were lucky enough to survive childhood, your average life expectancy was somewhere between twenty-five and forty, depending on your social class and gender. Many women, until the advent of modern medicine in the twentieth century, died in childbirth. Currently, the average American can expect to live to be seventy-eight. Up until very recent times, death for our ancestors was a common, everyday occurrence. Today, death is the domain of the very old or the very unfortunate.

The relative rarity of death in our lives today may explain our seemingly contradictory response to it. While popular culture is filled with an abundance of the fictional undead—vampires, werewolves, zombies, you name it— realistic depictions of actual death and dying are few and far between. Many of the most popular books, movies, and TV series of recent times feature the undead, such as HBO's *True Blood* series, AMC's *The Walking Dead*, or the hugely successful *Twilight* franchise. Actual death, however, has become a kind of cultural taboo. Individuals generally no longer die at home cared for by friends and family, but instead die in institutional surroundings, such as hospitals, nursing homes, and hospices. Very few films or TV series portray death as a normal, natural part of life. When real death is addressed, it is exceptional, dramatic, and often in the service of a social issue, such as cancer or AIDS, as in the films *The Bucket List* (2007), *Philadelphia* (1993), and *Wit* (2001). While the average American watches multiple fictional deaths each week through multi-media outlets—streaming video, DVD rentals, TV broadcasts, etc.—few people under thirty in this country have ever witnessed the actual death of another.

Some people may argue that our ignorance of death is a good thing—why not take advantage of modern life and continue to protect ourselves from the gruesome and painful reality of death? Yet death is a natural part of life, as natural as birth, which today is the occasion for celebration by family and friends, although it used to be as shrouded in mystery as death is today. In the past, it was considered impolite to refer to a woman as pregnant. People instead used a variety of euphemisms, such as "expecting," or "being in the family way," or the popular "with child." Nor was giving birth the public event it is today. In the past, women gave birth at home with a doctor or midwife in attendance. After WWI, it became common for women to give birth in the hospital, with friends and family—even fathers—prohibited from any participation in the process of birth itself. Today, most hospitals have separate facilities for labor and delivery in order to achieve a more welcoming, home-like atmosphere, with some women actually choosing to give birth at home. Giving birth is no longer seen as a kind of sickness, but instead as a natural, joyful process. Labor and delivery rooms look more like hotel suites, with space for children, parents, grandparents, and friends to witness the birth.

If our society can overcome the fear and shame that was once associated with giving birth, and instead transform it into a happy celebration, surely we can also come to a better understanding of death. As the readings here illustrate, acceptance of death as a normal part of life confers real emotional, financial, and social benefits.

Given our unease with death, this book includes a collection of works designed to demystify the topic for readers, especially the question of what happens to us when we die. Physician and scholar Elisabeth Kübler-Ross discusses our modern fears about death in a chapter from her influential book, *On Death and Dying*. Biologist Lewis Thomas provides a reassuring explanation of the merciful qualities of dying naturally in his essay "On Natural Death," while Constance Jones describes what actually happens to our consciousness as we die in her essay "The Dying Brain and Near-Death Experience." Mary Roach provides a graphic depiction of the natural process of decay in the excerpt from her book, *Stiff: The Curious Lives of Human Cadavers*, and is contrasted with Jessica Mitford's critique of the funeral industry in the excerpt from her book *The American Way of Death, Revisited*.

This collection also includes works by some of America's greatest writers on the experiences of loss, grief, and death, such as Audre Lorde's speech about her fight with cancer and the medical establishment titled "The Transformation of Silence into Language and Action." Also included is E. B. White's wonderful essay on mortality in "Once More to the Lake." Essays by Virginia Woolf and Annie Dillard, both on the subject of the death of a moth, use the lyrical gifts of the poet to evoke the themes of death and feminist liberation, while Mitch Albom provides readers with a moving portrait of his dying professor in an excerpt from *Tuesdays with Morrie*.

Other works included help extend the critical discussion of death, such as Jenna Wortham's article "As Facebook Users Die, Ghosts Reach Out" on death and social media, or Claire Lambrecht's interview of Ruth Davis Konigsberg, who pointedly critiques Elisabeth Kübler-Ross's work. Perhaps most controversial is Helen Prejean's real-life account of an execution, in an excerpt from her famous book *Dead Man Walking*.

To begin our discussion of society's peculiar attitude toward death, consider the following song lyrics by Ralph Stanley, Blue Öyster Cult, and Jars of Clay. Song lyrics, along with the music, images, and voice of the artist, create meaning for songs. Popular culture is a rich mine of attitudes and beliefs about many themes—death being only one. The lyrics of each song below make a statement about the topic. What do you think they say about death?

"O DEATH"
BY RALPH STANLEY

O, Death
O, Death
Won't you spare me over till another year
Well what is this that I can't see
With ice cold hands takin' hold of me
Well I am death, none can excel
I'll open the door to heaven or hell
Whoa, death someone would pray
Could you wait to call me another day
The children prayed, the preacher preached
Time and mercy is out of your reach
I'll fix your feet till you can't walk
I'll lock your jaw till you can't talk
I'll close your eyes so you can't see
This very air, come and go with me
I'm death I come to take the soul
Leave the body and leave it cold
To draw up the flesh off of the frame
Dirt and worm both have a claim
O, Death
O, Death
Won't you spare me over till another year
My mother came to my bed
Placed a cold towel upon my head
My head is warm my feet are cold
Death is a-movin' upon my soul
Oh, death how you're treatin' me
You've closed my eyes so I can't see
Well you're hurtin' my body
You make me cold

You run my life right outta my soul
Oh death please consider my age
Please don't take me at this stage
My wealth is all at your command
If you will move your icy hand
Oh the young, the rich or poor
Hunger like me you know
No wealth, no ruin, no silver no gold
Nothing satisfies me but your soul
O, death
O, death
Won't you spare me over till another year
Won't you spare me over till another year
Won't you spare me over till another year

"(DON'T FEAR) THE REAPER" BY BLUE ÖYSTER CULT

All our times have come
Here but now they're gone
Seasons don't fear the reaper
Nor do the wind, the sun or the rain
We can be like they are

Come on baby, don't fear the reaper
Baby take my hand, don't fear the reaper
We'll be able to fly, don't fear the reaper
Baby I'm your man

La la la la la
La la la la la

Valentine is done
Here but now they're gone
Romeo and Juliet
Are together in eternity
Romeo and Juliet

40,000 men and women every day
Like Romeo and Juliet
40,000 men and women every day
Redefine happiness
Another 40,000 coming every day
We can be like they are

Come on baby, don't fear the reaper
Baby take my hand, don't fear the reaper
We'll be able to fly, don't fear the reaper
Baby I'm your man

La la la la la
La la la la la

Love of two is one
Here but now they're gone
Came the last night of sadness
And it was clear she couldn't go on
Then the door was open and the wind appeared
The candles blew then disappeared
The curtains flew then he appeared, saying don't be afraid

Come on baby . . . and she had no fear
And she ran to him, then they started to fly
They looked backward and said goodbye
She had become like they are
She had taken his hand, she had become like they are
Come on baby . . . don't fear the reaper

"ALL MY TEARS"
BY JARS OF CLAY

When I go don't cry for me in my Father's arms I'll be
The wounds this world left on my soul will all be healed and I'll be whole.

Sun and moon will be replaced with the light of Jesus' face
And I will not be ashamed, for my Savior knows my name

It don't matter where you bury me, I'll be home and I'll be free
It don't matter where I lay, all my tears be washed away.

Gold and silver blind the eye, temporary riches lie
Come and eat from heaven's store, come and drink and thirst no more

It don't matter where you bury me, I'll be home and I'll be free
It don't matter where I lay, all my tears be washed away

So weep not for me my friends, when my time below does end
For my life belongs to Him, who will raise the dead again.

It don't matter where you bury me, 'cause I'll be home and I'll be free.
It don't matter where I lay, all my tears be washed away.

Ooh, it don't matter . . . Ooh, it don't matter.

xplore Choose one of the songs listed above. Using Google, Bing, or another search engine, find an audio or video performance of the song on a Web site, such as YouTube. Does the artist's performance change your interpretation of the song's lyrics? If so, how did it change? If not, why not, in your opinion?

aborate Working together in groups, compare the lyrics in these three songs. Identify the main speaker or speakers in each song. What do you think is the speaker's attitude toward death? Underline specific passages in each song to support your analysis. Are these attitudes alike? Are they different? Explain.

DEATH

Michael Sims has written and edited a variety of books, including Dracula's Guest: A Connoisseur's Collection of Victorian Vampire Stories. *His work often explores the relationship between nature and culture, and has appeared in such varied publications as the* Washington Post, *England's* New Statesman, *and* American Anthropology. *In this article, Sims speculates about the physical and scientific reasons that underlie our myths about the dead.*

ALL THE DEAD ARE VAMPIRES

BY MICHAEL SIMS

A NATURAL-HISTORICAL LOOK AT OUR LOVE-HATE RELATIONSHIP WITH DEAD PEOPLE.

I remember the view from a grave. Cartoon stars spiraled in front of my eyes when I hit the damp soil at the bottom. Up there on the faraway earth, past six feet of square muddy wall, a man and a boy stared down at me—my brothers, Gary and David, both laughing. Until I slipped and fell into the grave, we had been setting up the graveside for a funeral. Gary, 11 years older than I, worked for a funeral home; more than once in our childhood, David and I rode with him to pick up a corpse. I remember coming in the back door of a funeral home around midnight— the glare of fluorescent lights on stainless-steel tables, the smell of antiseptic, and another odor underneath. Only once did I actually zip up a body bag over a dead man's nose. Once was enough.

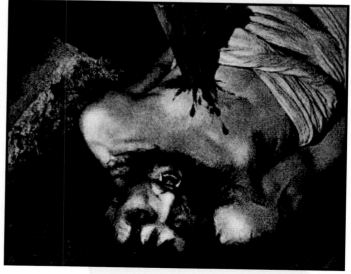

Bettman, Corbis

These mostly forgotten memories returned after I was invited last year to edit an anthology of vampire stories.

"Vampire stories?" I repeated. Despite a secret fascination with werewolves—something strikes home for me about the need for anger management to keep you from going all beastly during a crisis—I had never really been a fan of vampires. I wasn't reading the *Twilight* books or watching *True Blood*. I never even read *Interview With the Vampire*—even though I dated a psychic vampire back in the early 90s—and my Tom Cruise allergy kept me from the movie.

The editor clarified: "*Victorian* vampire stories."

"Oh, I see." He knows I have a weakness for the atmosphere of Victorian genre fiction, from Raffles relieving the aristocracy of the burden of wealth to pissed-off ghosts chasing M.R. James's bumbling antiquarians. Who can resist an era in which first aid for any trouble begins with a shout of, "Brandy! For God's sake, bring her some brandy!"

So, wondering how I would find a new angle on vampire stories, I said yes. Anthologizing is a dusty sport, half antique hunting and half literary gossipfest, and I love it. I went home and prowled my shelves and realized how many of the Victorian-era stories I had already read. Why, here's that pasty-faced bastard Lord Ruthven, by Byron's doctor and hanger-on, John Polidori, and so obviously based upon Byron himself. Here is Théophile Gautier's crazy priest, in love with a vampire courtesan and wrestling with his naughty soul. And there were many stories I hadn't read before—gay vampires, child vampires, even an invisible vampire.

To understand how this modern mythology blossomed during the Romantic and Victorian century, I had to go to the allegedly true 18th-century accounts of vampirism. With or without clergy, the citizenry often performed frenzied exhumations because they feared that Aunt Helga was returning to prey upon her relatives.

As I read about the careful inspection of corpses for signs of vampirism, a curious thing happened. Slowly I began to *get* vampire stories: the horror of our aspiring consciousness finding itself trapped in a mortal body, the threatening presence of the already deceased, even the undead's gamble on a kind of credit—another's blood instead of their own—rather than acceptance of normal human fate.

Reading about these fictional bodies—bodies of victims and of monsters—reminded me of bodies I had known. I remembered my own encounters with death, from riding in a hearse with a corpse strapped to a gurney behind us to sitting beside a friend's father in the hospital as he sighed his last breath. I remembered my momentary horror and panic when I fell into the grave. It wasn't like falling off a ladder. This was a *grave*.

As I worked on the introduction to the anthology, I merged the two main topics I write about: natural history and Victorian literature. I tried to look at vampires from a scientific point of view. After all, where did we get this fear that, once the sun goes down, the ghoulish undead climb out of their coffins and come back for the rest of us? It didn't emerge out of thin air.

The vampire story as we know it was born in the early 19th century, as the wicked love child of rural folklore and urban decadence. But in writing these depraved tales, Byron and Polidori and company were refining the raw ore of peasant superstition. And the peasant brain had simply been doing what the human brain does best: sorting information into explanatory narratives.

I found lots of reports of vampires from Europe—from urban France, rural Russia, the islands of Greece, the mountains of Romania. Along the way, I was reminded of something I already knew but hadn't thought of as relevant in this context: During the Middle Ages and Renaissance, dead bodies were a common sight. Plague and countless other illnesses ravaged every community. Corpses of the executed and tortured were displayed in public as warnings, even left hanging as they decomposed.

Few bodies seemed to rest peacefully even in the ground. Often people in the 18th century had an opportunity not only to see corpses but also to glimpse them again after they were buried. Urban cemeteries were densely overcrowded, sometimes with the dead stacked several graves deep, causing horrific spillage during floods or earthquakes. More corpses than the ground could accommodate resulted in the stench of decay and the constant risk of disease. Grave desecration was also common; a thriving trade in illicit cadavers for medical students joined a vicious rivalry between competing religious groups. After Louis XIV abolished the convent at Port-Royal des Champs as a hotbed of Jansenist heresy, drunken locals dug up nuns' bodies from the cemetery and fed them to their dogs. Corpses of executed heretics were dragged through the streets, then reburied in too-small graves by breaking the body into small pieces.

I found in older vampire stories that often the person who returns as a vampire was irreligious during life—irreverent, scornful of the infallibility of the church or the need for communion, for example. People worried especially about those who had been excommunicated and denied burial in a church-approved cemetery. If your soul didn't sleep peacefully in the arms of the Lord, what might it be up to?

In his 1746 compendium, *The Phantom World*, Augustin Calmet explored those questions. In a section headed "Do the excommunicated rot in the earth?," he examined the common fear that the body of a heretic does not decompose but instead lingers in the earth, profaning the laws of God in death as it did in life, polluting the ground with its sinfulness and disease. Unlikely comrades, such as natural philosophers and village priests, found themselves allied in an antipollution movement, lobbying for the segregation of cemeteries to rural areas beyond dense centers of population—where their rotting inhabitants could inflict less harm on the living.

The scholar Marie-Hélène Huet sums up the subtext of many early vampire accounts: "All the dead are vampires, poisoning the air, the blood, the life of the living, contaminating their body and their soul, robbing them of their sanity."

As I continued digging into the literature, I wondered: If ordinary people were encountering the corpses of the recently dead or even long-dead friends and relatives, what were they actually seeing that they misinterpreted and then wove into a vampire mythology? Not surprisingly, no one understood the process of decay within a subterranean chamber. They had no forensic body farm at which to chart a corpse's fade from nauseating stink to cautionary bones.

Any variation from "normal" in the grave provoked fear, yet there isn't really much of a norm in the process of decay under different circumstances. Some coffins protect their residents better than others. Lime helps preserve a body, as do clay soil and low humidity. Graves in different climates and latitudes vary, depending upon air temperature and humidity, soil composition, and insects, not to mention those invisible sanitation workers who turn us all back into the dust from which we came—and of course in the 18th century, no one knew that such creatures existed.

Many natural changes after death were judged to be evidence that the late lamented had turned into a bloodsucker. Like hair, fingernails don't actually continue to grow after death, but as fingers decompose, the skin shrinks, making the nails look abnormally long and clawlike. You begin to look as if you're turning into a predatory animal. Dead skin, after sloughing off its top layer, can look flushed and alive as if with fresh blood. Damp soil's chemicals can produce in the skin a waxy secretion, sometimes brownish or even white, from fat and protein—adipocere, "grave wax." In one eyewitness account from the 18th century, a vampire is even found—further proof of his vile nature— to have a certain region of his anatomy in a posthumous state of excitement. The genitals often inflate during the process of decomposition.

And what about the blood reported around the mouths of resurrected corpses? That too has a natural explanation. Without the heart as a pump to keep it circulating, blood follows the path of least resistance. Many bodies were buried face down, resulting in blood pooling in the face and leaving it looking flushed. Sometimes blood also gets lifted mouthward by gases from decomposition. Vampire stories recognize that death is messy.

Much of the original folklore does not include our familiar theme nowadays, that the undead recruit their own next generation by infecting victims when they drink their blood. Often I found the fear that a corpse might spontaneously transform into a vampire without ever once making an unwilling blood donation during life. Your behavior before death was more important because it might increase your odds of coming back as a vampire. Felons, especially murderers, were thought likelier to be cursed in this way—as were those poor souls presumptuous enough to commit suicide and take their departure schedule out of the hands of God.

Here's a list of other likely vampires: murderers' victims, the battlefield dead, the drowned, stroke victims, the first person to fall in an epidemic, heretics, wizards, alcoholics, grumpy people, women with questionable reputations, people who talk to themselves, and redheads.

Throughout my research, I found parallels between my own experience and vampire stories. When I read that list, I realized that the psychic vampire I once dated was a redhead. I'm just saying.

What I didn't foresee, when I signed on to compile an anthology of Victorian vampire stories, is that these tales from the dawn of the genre would tap into fears from the dawn of my own life, as well as more recent experiences. Once, in an emergency room, I was given an overdose of morphine for severe back pain. I flat-lined. My consciousness rushed away like an outgoing tide, and everything went black. I had just enough time to think, "Wow, dying is so easy." My wife recounts the next few minutes: a buzzer screaming, nurses racing in, calling to each other, giving me another injection, my EKG line getting excited again. Slowly I returned to consciousness, as if washing up on a beach. I shivered for days after that experience.

I didn't shiver like that again until late one night while reading Aleksey Tolstoy's "The Family of the Vourdalak." Gorcha, the grandfather of a village family, returns from 10 days in the mountains a disturbingly changed man, pale and slow. That evening he lures his own young grandson out into the darkness. I was reading this story late at night in the living room, with my wife already upstairs asleep. I began to shiver. I remembered my own grandfather's death when I was 7, how my memory of him merged with a late-night horror movie I had seen, how he kept coming back in my nightmares. In one dream, he limped up the gravel road from our family cemetery and tapped on my bedroom window. He wanted me to join him.

Of course he did; the dead always want us to join them. They frighten us because we know that someday we will see the view from a grave.

Michael Sims argues that literary depictions of the dead as vampires arose from our ancestors' experiences with the real dead. In the absence of scientific explanations, people imagined all sorts of reasons to explain how and why people died. Using Sims's logic, what real-life situations might account for the belief in ghosts, or witches, or even elves?

According to Sims, "The dead always want us to join them. They frighten us because we know that someday we will see the view from a grave." In a short essay (3–5 paragraphs) discuss your view of the dead. Are you afraid of dead bodies? Are you the kind of person who would be afraid to visit a funeral home, or do you love the thrill of the unknown? Do you find horror movies too scary, or do you find it all just silly and boring?

DEATH

Swiss American psychiatrist Elisabeth Kübler-Ross was a pioneer in near-death studies. This excerpt is from her groundbreaking book On Death and Dying *which established what is now referred to as the Kübler-Ross model for the five stages of death and grief: denial, anger, bargaining, depression, and acceptance. The chapter below outlines how modern society has come to view death as a frightening tragedy, rather than a natural event, like birth.*

excerpt from

ON DEATH AND DYING

BY ELISABETH KÜBLER-ROSS

ON THE FEAR OF DEATH

Let me not pray to be sheltered from
dangers but to be fearless in facing them.
Let me not beg for the stilling of
my pain but for the heart to conquer it.
Let me not look for allies in life's
battlefield but to my own strength.
Let me not crave in anxious fear to be saved
but hope for the patience to win my freedom.
Grant me that I may not be a coward,
feeling your mercy in my success alone;
but let me find the grasp
of your hand in my failure.

—Rabindranath Tagore,
Fruit-Gathering

Epidemics have taken a great toll of lives in past generations. Death in infancy and early childhood was frequent and there were few families who didn't lose a member of the family at an early age. Medicine has changed greatly in the last decades. Widespread vaccinations have practically eradicated many illnesses, at least in Western Europe and the United States. The use of chemotherapy, especially the antibiotics, has contributed to an ever decreasing number of fatalities in infectious diseases. Better child care and education had affected a low morbidity and mortality among children. The many diseases that have taken an impressive toll among the young and middle-aged have been conquered. The number of old people is on the rise, and with this fact come the number of people with malignancies and chronic diseases associated with old age.

Pediatricians have less work with acute and life-threatening situations as they have an ever increasing number of patients with psychosomatic disturbances and adjustment and behavior problems. Physicians have more people in their waiting rooms with emotional problems than they have ever had before, but they also have more elderly patients who not only try to live with their decreased physical abilities and limitations, but who also face loneliness and isolation with all its pains and anguish. The majority of these people are not seen by a psychiatrist. Their needs have to be elicited and gratified by other professional people, for instance, chaplains and social workers. It is for them that I am trying to outline the changes that have taken place in the last few decades, changes that are ultimately responsible for the increased fear of death, the rising number of emotional problems, and the greater need for understanding of and coping with the problems of death and dying.

When we look back in time and study old cultures and people, we are impressed that death has always been distasteful to man and will probably always be. From a psychiatrist's point of view this is very understandable and can perhaps best be explained by our basic knowledge that, in our unconscious, death is never possible in regard to ourselves. It is inconceivable for our unconscious to imagine an actual ending of our own life here on earth, and if this life of ours has to end, the ending is always attributed to a malicious intervention from the outside by someone else. In simple terms, in our unconscious mind we can only be killed; it is inconceivable to die of a natural cause or of old age. Therefore death in itself is associated with a bad act, a frightening happening, something that in itself calls for retribution and punishment.

One is wise to remember these fundamental facts as they are essential in understanding some of the most important, otherwise unintelligible communications of our patients.

The second fact that we have to comprehend is that in our unconscious mind we cannot distinguish between a wish and a deed. We are all aware of our illogical dreams in which two completely opposite statements can exist side by side—very acceptable in our dreams, but unthinkable and illogical in our wakening state. Just as our unconscious mind cannot differentiate between the wish to kill somebody in anger and the act of having done so, the young child is unable to make this distinction. The child who angrily wishes his mother to drop dead for not having gratified his needs will be traumatized greatly by the actual death of his mother—even if this event is not linked closely in time with his destructive wishes. He will always take part or the whole blame for the loss of his mother. He will always say to himself—rarely to others—"I did it, I am responsible, I was bad, therefore Mommy left me." It is well to remember that the child will react in the same manner if he loses a parent by divorce, separation, or desertion. Death is often seen by a child as an impermanent thing and has therefore little distinction from a divorce in which he may have an opportunity to see a parent again.

Many a parent will remember remarks of their children such as, "I will bury my doggy now and next spring when the flowers come up again, he will get up." Maybe it was the same wish that motivated the ancient Egyptians to supply their dead with food and goods to keep them happy and the old American Indians to bury their relatives with their belongings.

When we grow older and begin to realize that our omnipotence is really not so omnipotent, that our strongest wishes are not powerful enough to make the impossible possible, the fear that we have contributed to the death of a loved one diminishes—and with it the guilt. The fear remains diminished, however, only so long as it is not challenged too strongly. Its vestiges can be seen daily in hospital corridors and in people associated with the bereaved.

A husband and wife may have been fighting for years, but when the partner dies, the survivor will pull his hair, whine and cry louder and beat his chest in regret, fear and anguish, and will hence fear his own death more than before, still believing in the law of Talion—an eye for an eye, a tooth for a tooth—"I am responsible for her death, I will have to die a pitiful death in retribution."

Maybe this knowledge will help us understand many of the old customs and rituals which have lasted over the centuries and whose purpose is to diminish the anger of the gods or the people as the case may be, thus decreasing the anticipated punishment. I am thinking of the ashes, the torn clothes, the veil, the *Klage Weiber* of the old days—they are all means to ask you to take pity on them, the mourners, and are expressions of sorrow, grief, and shame. If someone grieves, beats his chest, tears his hair, or refuses to eat, it is an attempt at self-punishment to avoid or reduce the anticipated punishment for the blame that he takes on the death of a loved one.

This grief, shame, and guilt are not very far removed from feelings of anger and rage. The process of grief always includes some qualities of anger. Since none of us likes to admit anger at a deceased person, these emotions are often disguised or repressed and prolong the period of grief or show up in other ways. It is well to remember that it is not up to us to judge such feelings as bad or shameful, but to understand their true meaning and origin as something very human. In order to illustrate this I will again use the example of the child—and the child in us. The five-year-old who loses his mother is both blaming himself for her disappearance and being angry at her for having deserted him and for no longer gratifying his needs. The dead person then turns into something the child loves and wants very much but also hates with equal intensity for this severe deprivation.

The ancient Hebrews regarded the body of a dead person as something unclean and not to be touched. The early American Indians talked about the evil spirits and shot arrows in the air to drive the spirits away. Many other cultures have rituals to take care of the "bad" dead person, and they all originate in this wish to keep the bad spirits deep down in the ground, and the pebbles that many mourners put on the grave are left-over symbols of the same wish. Though we call the firing of guns at military funerals a last salute, it is the same symbolic ritual as the Indian used when he shot his spears and arrows into the skies.

I give these examples to emphasize that man has not basically changed. Death is still a fearful, frightening happening, and the fear of death is a universal fear even if we think we have mastered it on many levels.

What has changed is our way of coping and dealing with death and dying and our dying patients.

Having been raised in a country in Europe where science is not so advanced, where modern techniques have just started to find their way into medicine, and where people still live as they did in this country half a century ago, I may have had an opportunity to study a part of the evolution of mankind in a shorter period.

I remember as a child the death of a farmer. He fell from a tree and was not expected to live. He asked simply to die at home, a wish that was granted without questioning. He called his daughters into the bedroom and spoke with each one of them alone for a few minutes. He arranged his affairs quietly, though he was in great pain, and distributed his belongings and his land, none of which was to be split until his wife should follow him in death. He also asked each of his children to share in the work, duties, and tasks that he had carried on until the time of the accident. He asked his friends to visit him once more, to bid good-bye to them. Although I was a small child at the time, he did not exclude me or my siblings. We were allowed to share in the preparations of the family just as we were permitted to grieve with them until he died. When he did die, he was left at home, in his own beloved home which he had built, and among his friends and neighbors who went to take a last look at him where he lay in the midst of flowers in the place he had lived in and loved so much. In that country today there is still no make-believe slumber room, no embalming, no false makeup to pretend sleep. Only the signs of very disfiguring illnesses are covered up with bandages and only infectious cases are removed from the home prior to the burial.

Why do I describe such "old-fashioned" customs? I think they are an indication of our acceptance of a fatal outcome, and they help the dying patient as well as his family to accept the loss of a loved one. If a patient is allowed to terminate his life in the familiar and beloved environment, it requires less adjustment for him. His own family knows him well enough to replace a sedative with a glass of his favorite wine; or the smell of a home-cooked soup may give him the appetite to sip a few spoons of fluid which, I think, is still more enjoyable than an infusion. I will not minimize the need for sedatives and infusions and realize full well from my own experience as a country doctor that they are sometimes life-saving and often unavoidable. But I also know that patience and familiar people and food could replace many a bottle of intravenous fluids given for the simple reason that it fulfills the physiological need without involving too many people and/or individual nursing care.

The fact that children are allowed to stay at home where a fatality has stricken and are included in the talk, discussions, and fears gives them the feeling that they are not alone in the grief and gives them the comfort of shared responsibility and shared mourning. It prepares them gradually and helps them view death as part of life, an experience which may help them grow and mature.

This is in great contrast to a society in which death is viewed as taboo, discussion of it is regarded as morbid, and children are excluded with the presumption and pretext that it would be "too much" for them. They are then sent off to relatives, often accompanied with some unconvincing lies of "Mother has gone on a long trip" or other unbelievable stories. The child senses that something is wrong, and his distrust in adults will only multiply if other relatives add new variations of the story, avoid his questions or suspicions, shower him with gifts as a meager substitute for a loss he is not permitted to deal with. Sooner or later the child will become aware of the changed family situation and, depending on the age and personality of the child, will have an unresolved grief and regard this incident as a frightening, mysterious, in any case very traumatic experience with untrustworthy grownups, which he has no way to cope with.

It is equally unwise to tell a little child who lost her brother that God loved little boys so much that he took little Johnny to heaven. When this little girl grew up to be a woman she never solved her anger at God, which resulted in a psychotic depression when she lost her own little son three decades later.

We would think that our great emancipation, our knowledge of science and of man, has given us better ways and means to prepare ourselves and our families for this inevitable happening. Instead the days are gone when a man was allowed to die in peace and dignity in his own home.

The more we are making advancements in science, the more we seem to fear and deny the reality of death. How is this possible?

We use euphemisms, we make the dead look as if they were asleep, we ship the children off to protect them from the anxiety and turmoil around the house if the patient is fortunate enough to die at home, we don't allow children to visit their dying parents in the hospitals, we have long and controversial discussions about whether patients should be told the truth—a question that rarely arises when the dying person is tended by the family physician who has known him from delivery to death and who knows the weaknesses and strengths of each member of the family.

I think there are many reasons for this flight away from facing death calmly. One of the most important facts is that dying nowadays is more gruesome in many ways, namely, more lonely, mechanical, and dehumanized; at times it is even difficult to determine technically when the time of death has occurred.

Dying becomes lonely and impersonal because the patient is often taken out of his familiar environment and rushed to an emergency room. Whoever has been very sick and has required rest and comfort especially may recall his experience of being put on a stretcher and enduring the noise of the ambulance siren and hectic rush until the hospital gates open. Only those who have lived through this may appreciate the discomfort and cold necessity of such transportation which is only the beginning of a long ordeal—hard to endure when you are well, difficult to express in words when noise, light, pumps, and voices are all too much to put up with. It may well be that we might consider more the patient under the sheets and blankets and perhaps stop our well-meant efficiency and rush in order to hold the patient's hand, to smile, or to listen to a question. I include the trip to the hospital as the first episode in dying, as it is for many. I am putting it exaggeratedly in contrast to the sick man who is left at home—not to say that lives should not be saved if they can be saved by a hospitalization, but to keep the focus on the patient's experience, his needs and his reactions.

When a patient is severely ill, he is often treated like a person with no right to an opinion. It is often someone else who makes the decision if and when and where a patient should be hospitalized. It would take so little to remember that the sick person too has feelings, has wishes and opinions, and has—most important of all—the right to be heard.

Well, our presumed patient has now reached the emergency room. He will be surrounded by busy nurses, orderlies, interns, residents, a lab technician perhaps who will take some blood, an electrocardiogram technician who takes the cardiogram. He may be moved to X-ray and he will overhear opinions of his condition and discussions and questions to members of the family. He slowly but surely is beginning to be treated like a thing. He is no longer a person. Decisions are made often without his opinion. If he tries to rebel he will be sedated and after hours of waiting and wondering whether he has the strength, he will be wheeled into the operating room or intensive treatment unit and become an object of great concern and great financial investment.

He may cry for rest, peace, and dignity, but he will get infusions, transfusions, a heart machine, or tracheostomy if necessary. He may want one single person to stop for one single minute so that he can ask one single question— but he will get a dozen people around the clock, all busily preoccupied with his heart rate, pulse, electrocardiogram or pulmonary functions, his secretions or excretions but not with him as a human being. He may wish to fight it all but it is going to be a useless fight since all this is done in the fight for his life, and if they can save his life they can consider the person afterwards. Those who consider the person first may lose precious time to save his life! At least this seems to be the rationale or justification behind all this—or is it? Is the reason for this increasingly mechanical, depersonalized approach our own defensiveness? Is this approach our own way to cope with and repress the anxieties that a terminally or critically ill patient evokes in us? Is our concentration on equipment, on blood pressure our desperate attempt to deny the impending death which is so frightening and discomforting to us that we displace all our knowledge onto machines, since they are less close to us than the suffering face of another human being which would remind us once more of our lack of omnipotence, our own limits and failures, and last but not least perhaps our own mortality?

Maybe the question has to be raised: Are we becoming less human or more human? Though this book is in no way meant to be judgmental, it is clear that whatever the answer may be, the patient is suffering more—not physically, perhaps, but emotionally. And his needs have not changed over the centuries, only our ability to gratify them.

Elisabeth Kübler-Ross argues that our society has come to view death as something of a taboo, where "discussion of it is regarded as morbid, and children are excluded with the presumption and pretext that it would be 'too much' for them." Do you agree here with her claim? Were you ever, as a child, sheltered from the reality of death? Do you think children today are protected from experiencing death?

Working together in groups, identify the claim or claims Kübler-Ross makes about our view of death and dying. What reasons does she provide in support of her claims? What evidence does she include to support her reasons and claims? Does your group find her argument persuasive?

Operating under the assumption that popular culture reflects a society's values and concerns, find three current general magazines, journals, or newspapers (online or in print) and examine them for articles on death and dying. How many items did you find? If Kübler-Ross is correct in her analysis of our attitude toward death, how many would you expect to find?

Taboo or not, all of us come to experience death at some point in our lives. Write a short essay (3–5 paragraphs) about an experience you have had with death. Did your experience support Kübler-Ross's claims about our society's view of death?

DEATH

Journalist Ruth Davis Konigsberg is a senior editor at Time, *as well as the author of* The Truth about Grief: The Myth of Its Five Stages and the New Science of Loss. *In this interview conducted by Claire Lambrecht, she critiques Elisabeth Kübler-Ross's theory on the stages of grief.*

THE TRUTH ABOUT GRIEF: WHAT'S WRONG WITH A NATION OF MOURNERS?

BY CLAIRE LAMBRECHT

Our once-stoic culture has embraced public grief. An expert explains why it might be getting in the way of recovery.

"It's my job to get them to acceptance," says Steve Carell's character Michael Scott on "The Office," before launching into a session of unsolicited grief counseling. "And if not acceptance, then just depression. If I can get them depressed, then I'll have done my job."

There were days when Michael Scott's advocacy could have been seen as subversive. It certainly was for Sally Field's character in the 1989 film "Steel Magnolias." "Maybe I should have an emotional outburst more often," she says toward the end of the film, defending a torrent that erupts after two hours of soft-spoken timidity. In many ways, the movement from Sally Field to Michael Scott demonstrates a significant shift in American consciousness. When it comes to grief and loss, America is no longer a nation of stoics; we are a nation of feelers.

It's evidence of what a profound effect Elisabeth Kübler-Ross' five stages of grief—denial, anger, bargaining, depression and acceptance—have had on our culture, ever since Kübler-Ross first identified them in 1969. "You must get it out. Grief must be witnessed to be healed," Kübler-Ross wrote in the 2005 book "On Grief and Grieving." And boy, has our grief found witnesses, from guilty-pleasure reality television like "The Bachelor" and manic audition lines for "American Idol" to acclaimed memoirs like Joan Didion's "The Year of Magical Thinking."

But are all these public displays of emotion really helping? Modern research suggests that may not be the case, as Ruth Davis Konigsberg finds in her eminently readable and intelligent new book "The Truth About Grief." A journalist and former New York magazine editor, Konigsberg investigates how Kübler-Ross's theories weaseled their way into the American psyche—and how we might dig ourselves out again.

Salon sat down with Konigsberg last week to get, as she puts it, the truth about grief.

How did the Kübler-Ross model of grieving become so popular?

The stages of grief hold great appeal because they give us a sense of control over a difficult experience, a sort of a road map. But their popularity tells us more about ourselves and the way we like to order things than it does about grief. Stages are everywhere: "The 9 Steps to Financial Freedom," "The 7 Habits of Highly Effective People." It's all part of the same idea.

Which is?

The idea—I call it Stageism, and it was fueled by the self-help movement—is that any problem can not only be tackled with a series of steps but provides an opportunity for personal growth. It's a way of simplifying life's challenges and implies a reward for suffering. If only things were so!

What are the defining characteristics of grief in American culture?

Aside from the stages, there is a lot of emphasis on the expression of negative emotions. But recent studies have shown that people who express those emotions, or do their "grief work," don't heal any faster. Studies even show that talking or writing about one's loss isn't necessarily helpful.

Would you say, then, that the idea of catharsis and the whole "you have to get it out" mentality is a myth?

Not exactly. It depends upon the problem or situation you're trying to ameliorate. Psychotherapy has been proven effective for treating clinical depression, not just sadness and anxiety, although that may be more because it helps someone identify and change destructive thought patterns. But "catharsis" certainly isn't always the answer. Some people might not be comfortable with a public airing of emotion; others might exhibit more "repressive coping" where they are able to modulate their negative emotions, which, contrary to the notion of catharsis, seems to have a protective function.

Yet there is still huge attention paid to public grieving.

In a way, we have become spectators and kind of consumers of other people's grief. With the Internet, all of these grief blogs, and grief memoirs. Kübler-Ross said, "Grief must be witnessed in order to heal. You have to get it out." And everyone's getting it out. There is something very poignant and very captivating about reading or hearing about somebody else's loss, but this trend also shows the level of public expression that grief has reached today.

Has it always been this way?

I chart the history of that a bit. After the Civil War and into the Victorian Age, the public expression of grief peaked. It went down after World War I for various political and historical reasons, and now I feel like we're at another sort of peak. It's very interesting, because what a lot of these grief memoirists say is, "Well, grief is taboo, and nobody wants to hear about your grief." I feel like back in the 1950s that was probably true. And that was a very good reason for the death and dying movement to crack that whole thing open and start a discussion about death and dying. That was a good reaction to a repressive and stoic culture. Now we have the opposite culture, which is expressive and not stoic, yet they continue to reiterate this idea that grief is taboo. It's obviously anything but taboo. That's like saying sex is taboo. It's like, really, are you kidding me?

What do most people misunderstand about grieving?

"If you don't get it all out, then it's going to fester." The idea of delayed grief has been debunked by research. People who did well after a short time did not decline later. There is no evidence of the delayed grief phenomenon. People who do well early on tend to do well later. The way it is portrayed is a uniform state, but temperament almost has more predictive value than anything else.

I want to give people a helpful message. There is no one thing you have to do. The truth is you probably already have what you need to get through loss.

Can you expand on this a little bit?

There are several different ways people might grieve, and researchers are now identifying patterns in responses, so that there is no one prescription one should follow—the five stages being the most well-known, but there are others out there as well.

How does America compare to other cultures. What do we have to learn?

I chose to look at certain indigenous healing practices that you could find in places in China, and also in the Chinese-American communities here in the U.S., because they provide such a contrast to our own approach. We think that our approach is natural and instinctive and therefore the best way, when, in fact, it's based on our own notions of mental health, which the rest of the world might not share.

I talked to this one researcher, Paul Rosenblatt, who did a survey across all cultures. He basically said that there are no universal emotions to grief, not even crying. I don't know that we should necessarily adapt another culture's approach. Hopefully, our approach will evolve. Knowing that there are other approaches, and that this is all culturally relative, may free us from thinking that there is only one way.

Konigsberg claims that the repressed, "stoic" attitude toward death in 1950s America that Kübler-Ross's work helped open up has now gone to the opposite extreme, with public grieving the norm. What do you think about how we, as Americans, cope with grief?

Konigsberg challenges Elisabeth Kübler-Ross's ideas about the stages of grief, arguing that our often public expressions of grief are culturally—not psychologically—motivated. Using the resources of your campus library and/or the Internet, examine how other cultures express grief.

DEATH

THIS CITY IS BECOMING UNLIVEABLE

By David Sipress

"This city is becoming unlivable."

DEATH

Best-selling author and journalist Mitch Albom began Tuesdays with Morrie as a way to help his former professor, dying of ALS, pay his medical bills. The memoir spent four years on the New York Times Best Seller list and inspired a 1999 made-for-TV movie starring Jack Lemmon and Hank Azaria.

excerpt from

TUESDAYS WITH MORRIE

By Mitch Albom

THE AUDIOVISUAL

It is our first class together, in the spring of 1976. I enter Morrie's large office and notice the seemingly countless books that line the wall, shelf after shelf. Books on sociology, philosophy, religion, psychology. There is a large rug on the hardwood floor and a window that looks out on the campus walk. Only a dozen or so students are there, fumbling with notebooks and syllabi. Most of them wear jeans and earth shoes and plaid flannel shirts. I tell myself it will not be easy to cut a class this small. Maybe I shouldn't take it.

"Mitchell?" Morrie says, reading from the attendance list.

I raise a hand.

"Do you prefer Mitch? Or is Mitchell better?"

I have never been asked this by a teacher. I do a double take at this guy in his yellow turtleneck and green corduroy pants, the silver hair that falls on his forehead. He is smiling.

Mitch, I say. Mitch is what my friends called me.

"Well, Mitch it is then," Morrie says, as if closing a deal. "And Mitch?"

Yes?

"I hope that one day you will think of me as your friend."

THE ORIENTATION

As I turned the rental car onto Morrie's street in West Newton, a quiet suburb of Boston, I had a cup of coffee in one hand and a cellular phone between my ear and shoulder. I was talking to a TV producer about a piece we were doing. My eyes jumped from the digital clock—my return flight was in a few hours—to the mailbox numbers on the tree-lined suburban street. The car radio was on the all-news station. This was how I operated, five things at once.

"Roll back the tape," I said to the producer. "Let me hear that part again."

"Okay," he said. "It's gonna take a second."

Suddenly, I was upon the house. I pushed the brakes, spilling coffee in my lap. As the car stopped, I caught a glimpse of a large Japanese maple tree and three figures sitting near it in the driveway, a young man and a middle-aged woman flanking a small old man in a wheelchair.

Morrie.

At the sight of my old professor, I froze.

"Hello?" the producer said in my ear. "Did I lose you? . . ."

I had not seen him in sixteen years. His hair was thinner, nearly white, and his face was gaunt. I suddenly felt unprepared for this reunion—for one thing, I was stuck on the phone—and I hoped that he hadn't noticed my arrival, so that I could drive around the block a few more times, finish my business, get mentally ready. But Morrie, this new, withered version of a man I had once known so well, was smiling at the car, hands folded in his lap, waiting for me to emerge.

"Hey?" the producer said again. "Are you there?"

For all the time we'd spent together, for all the kindness and patience Morrie had shown me when I was young, I should have dropped the phone and jumped from the car, run and held him and kissed him hello.

Instead, I killed the engine and sunk down off the seat, as if I were looking for something.

"Yeah, yeah, I'm here," I whispered, and continued my conversation with the TV producer until we were finished.

I did what I had become best at doing: I tended to my work, even while my dying professor waited on his front lawn. I am not proud of this, but that is what I did.

Now, five minutes later, Morrie was hugging me, his thinning hair rubbing against my cheek. I had told him I was searching for my keys, that's what I had taken me so long in the car, and I squeezed him tighter, as if I could crush my little lie. Although the spring sunshine was warm, he wore a windbreaker and his legs were covered by a blanket. He smelled faintly sour, the way people on medication sometimes do. With his face pressed close to mine, I could hear his labored breathing in my ear.

"My old friend," he whispered, "you've come back at last."

He rocked against me, not letting go, his hands reaching up for my elbows as I bent over him. I was surprised at such affection after all these years, but then, in the stone walls I had built between my present and my past, I had forgotten how close we once were. I remembered graduation day, the briefcase, his tears at my departure, and I swallowed because I knew, deep down, that I was no longer the good, gift-bearing student he remembered.

I only hoped that, for the next few hours, I could fool him.

Inside the house, we sat at a walnut dining room table, near a window that looked out on the neighbor's house. Morrie fussed with his wheelchair, trying to get comfortable. As was his custom, he wanted to feed me, and I said all right. One of the helpers, a stout Italian woman named Connie, cut up bread and tomatoes and brought containers of chicken salad, hummus, and tabouli.

She also brought some pills. Morrie looked at them and sighed. His eyes were more sunken than I remembered them, and his cheekbones more pronounced. This gave him a harsher, older look—until he smiled, of course, and the sagging cheeks gathered up like curtains.

"Mitch," he said softly, "you know that I'm dying."

I knew.

"All right, then." Morrie swallowed the pills, put down the paper cup, inhaled deeply, then let it out. "Shall I tell you what it's like?"

What it's like? To die?

"Yes," he said.

Although I was unaware of it, our last class had just begun.

It is my freshman year. Morrie is older than most of the teachers, and I am younger than most of the students, having left high school a year early. To compensate for my youth on campus, I wear old gray sweatshirts and box in a local gym and walk around with an unlit cigarette in my mouth, even though I do not smoke. I drive a beat-up Mercury Cougar, with the windows down and the music up. I seek my identity in toughness—but it is Morrie's softness that draws me, and because he does not look at me as a kid trying to be something more than I am, I relax.

I finish that first course with him and enroll for another. He is an easy marker; he does not much care for grades. One year, they say, during the Vietnam War, Morrie gave all his male students A's to help them keep their student deferments.

I begin to call Morrie "Coach," the way I used to address my high school track coach. Morrie likes the nickname.

"Coach," he says. "All right, I'll be your coach. And you can be my player. You can play all the lovely parts of life that I'm too old for now."

Sometimes we eat together in the cafeteria. Morrie, to my delight, is even more of a slob than I am. He talks instead of chewing, laughs with his mouth open, delivers a passionate thought through a mouthful of egg salad, the little yellow pieces spewing from his teeth.

In cracks me up. The whole time I know him, I have two overwhelming desires: to hug him and to give him a napkin.

THE CLASSROOM

The sun beamed in through the dining room window, lighting up the hardwood floor. We had been talking there for nearly two hours. The phone rang yet again and Morrie asked his helper, Connie, to get it. She had been jotting the callers' names in Morrie's small black appointment book. Friends. Meditation teachers. A discussion group. Someone who wanted to photograph him for a magazine. It was clear I was not the only one interested in visiting my old professor—the "Nightline" appearance had made him something of a celebrity—but I was impressed with, perhaps even a bit envious of, all the friends that Morrie seemed to have. I thought about the "buddies" that circled my orbit back in college. Where had they gone?

"You know, Mitch, now that I'm dying, I've become much more interesting to people."

You were always interesting.

"Ho." Morrie smiled. "You're kind."

No, I'm not, I thought.

"Here's the thing," he said. "People see me as a bridge. I'm not as alive as I used to be, but I'm not yet dead. I'm sort of . . . in-between."

He coughed, then regained his smile. "I'm on the last great journey here— and people want me to tell them what to pack."

The phone rang again.

"Morrie, can you talk?" Connie asked.

"I'm visiting with my old pal now," he announced. "Let them call back."

I cannot tell you why he received me so warmly. I was hardly the promising student who had left him sixteen years earlier. Had it not been for "Nightline," Morrie might have died without ever seeing me again. I had no good excuse for this, except the one that everyone these days seems to have. I had become too wrapped up in the siren song of my own life. I was busy.

What happened to me? I asked myself. Morrie's high, smoky voice took me back to my university years, when I thought rich people were evil, a shirt and tie were prison clothes, and life without freedom to get up and go—motorcycle beneath you, breeze in your face, down the streets of Paris, into the mountains of Tibet—was not a good life at all. *What happened to me?*

The eighties happened. The nineties happened. Death and sickness and getting fat and going bald happened. I traded lots of dreams for a bigger paycheck, and I never even realized I was doing it.

Yet here was Morrie talking with the wonder of our college years, as if I'd simply been on a long vacation.

"Have you found someone to share your heart with?" he asked.

"Are you giving to your community?"

"Are you at peace with yourself?"

"Are you trying to be as human as you can be?"

I squirmed, wanting to show I had been grappling deeply with such questions. *What happened to me?* I once promised myself I would never work for money, that I would join the Peace Corps, that I would live in beautiful, inspirational places.

Instead, I had been in Detroit for ten years now, at the same workplace, using the same bank, visiting the same barber. I was thirty-seven, more efficient than in college, tied to computers and modems and cell phones. I wrote articles about rich athletes who, for the most part, could not care less about people like me. I was no longer young for my peer group, nor did I walk around in gray sweatshirts with unlit cigarettes in my mouth. I did not have long discussions over egg salad sandwiches about the meaning of life.

My days were full, yet I remained, much of the time, unsatisfied.

What happened to me?

"Coach," I said suddenly, remembering the nickname.

Morrie beamed. "That's me, I'm still your coach."

He laughed and resumed his eating, a meal he had started forty minutes earlier. I watched him now, his hands working gingerly, as if he were learning to use them for the very first time. He could not press down hard with a knife.

His fingers shook. Each bite was a struggle; he chewed the food finely before swallowing, and sometimes it slid out the sides of his lips, so that he had to put down what he was holding to dab his face with a napkin. The skin from his wrist to his knuckles was dotted with age spots, and it was loose, like skin hanging from a chicken soup bone.

For a while, we just ate like that, a sick old man, a healthy, younger man, both absorbing the quiet of the room. I would say it was an embarrassed silence, but I seemed to be the only one embarrassed.

"Dying," Morrie suddenly said, "is only one thing to be sad over, Mitch. Living unhappily is something else. So many of the people who come to visit me are unhappy."

Why?

"Well, for one thing, the culture we have does not make people feel good about themselves. We're teaching the wrong things. And you have to be strong enough to say if the culture doesn't work, don't buy it. Create your own. Most people can't do it. They're more unhappy than me—even in my current condition.

"I may be dying, but I am surrounded by loving, caring souls. How many people can say that?"

I was astonished by his complete lack of self-pity. Morrie, who could no longer dance, swim, bathe, or walk; Morrie, who could no longer answer his own door, dry himself after a shower, or even roll over in bed. How could he be so accepting? I watched him struggle with his fork, picking at a piece of tomato, missing it the first two times—a pathetic scene, and yet I could not deny that sitting in his presence was almost magically serene, the same calm breeze that soothed me back in college.

I shot a glance at my watch—force of habit—it was getting late, and I thought about changing my plane reservation home. Then Morrie did something that haunts me to this day.

"You know how I'm going to die?" he said.

I raised my eyebrows.

"I'm going to suffocate. Yes. My lungs, because of my asthma, can't handle the disease. It's moving up my body, this ALS. It's already got my legs. Pretty soon it'll get my arms and hands. And when it hits my lungs . . ."

He shrugged his shoulders.

" . . . I'm sunk."

I had no idea what to say, so I said, "Well, you know, I mean . . . you never know."

Morrie closed his eyes. "I know, Mitch. You mustn't be afraid of my dying. I've had a good life, and we all know it's going to happen. I maybe have four or five months."

Come on, I said nervously. Nobody can say—

"I can," he said softly. "There's even a little test. A doctor showed me."

A test?

"Inhale a few times."

I did as he said.

"Now, once more, but this time, when you exhale, count as many numbers as you can before you take another breath."

I quickly exhaled the numbers. "One-two-three-four-five-six-seven-eight . . ." I reached seventy before my breath was gone.

"Good," Morrie said, "You have healthy lungs. Now. Watch what I do."

He inhaled, then began his number count in a soft, wobbly voice. "One-two-three-four-five-six-seven-eight-nine-ten-eleven-twelve-thirteen-fourteen-fifteen-sixteen-seventeen-eighteen—"

He stopped, gasping for air.

"When the doctor first asked me to do this, I could reach twenty-three. Now it's eighteen."

He closed his eyes, shook his head. "My tank is almost empty."

I tapped my thighs nervously. That was enough for one afternoon.

"Come back and see your old professor," Morrie said when I hugged him good-bye.

I promised I would, and I tried not to think about the last time I promised this.

Mitch Albom writes of his conversations with a beloved former professor who was dying of ALS. If you could choose anyone in the world to share his or her final reflections before leaving this world, who would it be? What kind of insight would you hope to gain from this particular person?

Tuesdays with Morrie is a best-selling book of nonfiction. Using the resources of your local library, and/or the Internet, read a number of reviews of the book. What is it about this work that readers value? Why is it so popular?

DEATH

Actor Rainn Wilson, along with Devon Gundry, Golriz Lucina, and Shabnam Mogharabi, created Soulpancake in 2008. This unique and interactive Web site allows people from all walks of life to chime in on some of life's most philosophical questions.

excerpt from

SOULPANCAKE

BY RAINN WILSON, DEVON GUNDRY, GOLRIZ LUCINA, AND SHABNAM MOGHARABI

NEARLY 800 NEAR-DEATH EXPERIENCES HAPPEN EVERY DAY IN THE UNITED STATES.

SOURCE: NEAR DEATH EXPERIENCE RESEARCH FOUNDATION

THE NUMBER OF CREMATIONS IN THE UNITED STATES IS FORECAST TO DOUBLE TO ABOUT HALF OF ALL DEATHS BY 2020.

SOURCE: *St. Petersburg Times*

"DEATH IS NO MORE THAN PASSING FROM ONE ROOM INTO ANOTHER. BUT THERE'S A DIFFERENCE FOR ME, YOU KNOW. BECAUSE IN THAT OTHER ROOM I SHALL BE ABLE TO SEE." // **HELEN KELLER**

What do you hope happens when you die?

191

DIG DEEPER

WHY ARE WE SO AFRAID OF DEATH?

WHAT ONE QUESTION WOULD YOU WANT TO ASK A PERSON WHO RECENTLY DIED?

IF THERE'S NO LIFE AFTER DEATH, DO YOU WANT TO LIVE FOREVER?

"FROM MY ROTTING BODY, FLOWERS SHALL GROW AND I AM IN THEM AND THAT IS ETERNITY." // **EDVARD MUNCH**

Soulpancake is a unique blend of the philosophical with the arts. The artwork photographed above was created in response to the quotation by Edvard Munch, included on the page: "From my rotting body, flowers shall grow and I am in them and that is eternity." What do you think Munch meant by this quotation? Do you think the artwork and the words reflect or inspire one another? Explain.

Helen Keller's idea that the transition from life to death is no more than "passing from one room into another" indicates she had little fear of death. Working together in groups, search the Web for more quotations about death from other famous people. How many different sentiments about death did you find?

In a short essay (3-4 paragraphs) answer the question that is included in the artwork on the previous page: "What do you hope happens when you die?"

DEATH

Originally a costume and set designer, writer Anna Belle Kaufman became an art psychotherapist after the death of her five-year-old son from AIDS. In the article below, Kaufman relates the effect of her son's death on her and her family.

THINGS THAT WENT BUMP IN THE NIGHT

By Anna Belle Kaufman

A GRIEVING MOTHER HANGS ON FOR A HAUNTING

When I was six or seven, I didn't fear the monsters under the bed. My bogeyman was a book. Feeling a chill of fright if I so much as glanced at the worn gray-green binding, I knew the spot in my parents' bookcase where it lay in wait. The volume was a 19th-century collection of Hans Christian Andersen illustrated with sentimental engravings. Many of the tales had a dark and creepy tinge, but one story in particular frightened me and caused my aversion to the entire book. It was about a mother, weeping at her boy's graveside in the middle of the night, who sees a cloaked spectral figure:

> "You wish to go down to your child! Do you dare to follow me? I am Death." She assents, is enveloped in his mantle of darkness, and sinks down "deeper than the spade of the gravedigger can reach." The name of the story is "The Child in the Grave."

Thirty years later, on a hot Sunday in August 1986, sun floods our living room through a wall of windows. I am setting the table for brunch and waiting for the results of a blood test. In the yard I scan the redwood play structure with its yellow slide, the red trike parked on the brick patio, a child-size garden hoe and shovel propped against a post. I think I also see a ghostly form, a faint, ominous gray-green mist that flows and reconfigures itself, hovers, peers in the windows, tentatively touches the bell on the tricycle, sits on the swings.

My son, Zack, almost 4, is happily pushing small trains—his grand passion—along their wooden tracks in his bedroom when the grandparents arrive. Grandpa carries his instrument case and music. We are having our usual Sunday brunch with chamber music afterward—a trio, with Grandpa on flute, Grandma on the piano, my husband playing oboe. Zack likes to conduct the music with his dad's baton or draw while I listen and wash the dishes.

Zack loves drawing as much as I do. Obsessed with trains, Zack drew train tracks at two and a half. Now, he draws and paints his stuffed panda, Bumby, and endless pictures of tracks and trains complete with cowcatchers, engineers, and spewing smoke. A special train, "For my Momma," has pink hearts drifting out of the smokestack.

I do not tell my mother and father that we are waiting to hear whether their only grandchild has a deadly virus. I want them to have this last Sunday of music as usual.

Three days ago, when we took Zack to the hospital for the blood draw, our doctors said, "Don't worry, he can't have it." He is their success story—their interventions and ministrations have saved a child who almost died several times in his first two years. Zack spent so much time at Cedars-Sinai that everyone on the fourth floor knows the boy with the irresistible smile. The doctors don't want to find out that the treatments that saved his life will end it.

I, however, know the answer. After the blood test, I awakened at 3 a.m. and put it all together: transfusions and Zack's mysterious symptoms—lack of growth, constant infections, thrush, swollen glands, persistent diarrhea. I sat up and woke my husband. "Zack has AIDS." He listened skeptically and went back to sleep. I did not.

Zack is bent over paper and markers. My husband and my parents are playing Bach, unaware of the ghostly banshee hovering outside, patiently waiting, stroking the chains of Zack's swing. It is surreal to watch this child whose eyes dance under his shiny brown bangs and know that he is doomed.

Some days the ghoul thickens to clog the space between me and everything I experience, from fixing breakfast to tucking Zack into bed. At other times, the mist thins or wafts to the edges, seen only in my peripheral vision.

When school starts in the fall, no one knows about Zack's diagnosis except the principal. She and I want to spare a child who charms everyone he meets from becoming an object of fear and repugnance.

A year later, 1987, Zack is too ill to attend kindergarten. On a still night in Los Angeles, I hear Zack cry out and enter his room. I click the balloon man from night light to lamp. Red, yellow, white, and royal blue globes float into the rectangle of black glass. My pale, worried face, its wreath of dark curls melted into the blackness of the night window, appears above as another, larger balloon, untethered from the bundle.

I feel the heat rising from his forehead before I touch him. The pink and green cars printed on the pillowcase are dark with damp. His bangs are black shards stuck to his forehead, his eyes glassy and distant. Clutching Bumby's nose tightly with one hand, he points to the underside of the top bunk with the other. He must be delirious because he says, terrified, "Momma, look! There are monsters!" I wonder what he sees. Has delirium transmuted the jacquard weave of the satin mattress cover from curling vines to rampant beasts?

I climb in bed next to him until he falls asleep and then mount the ladder to the top bunk, where I spend the rest of the night on monster watch. He sleeps fitfully, still has a high fever the next day. He talks about the monsters coming back and dreads their return at nightfall. What can I do?

Suddenly an inspiration. Several days earlier, a friend stopped by and handed me a tiny brown vial filled with oil of lavender, explaining that the scent is relaxing and might be good for Zack. I forgot about it until now. I bring the bottle into Zack's room and explain that I have brought monster repellent to protect him when it gets dark.

"Pumpkin, you know how we use bug repellent to keep the mosquitoes away? How they don't bite us when they smell the repellent? Well, this works the same way. All I have to do is sprinkle it on your pillow and the monsters will smell it and run away." He nods assent, silently watching me. I place a cool compress on his forehead, and he closes his eyes and rubs Bumby's nose.

It works. The monsters flee and he is soothed to sleep by the aroma of lavender. We use the repellent for several nights until the fever is down. He is reassured by the little brown bottle that sits on the base of the balloon man lamp, at hand should the beasts return. They never do.

My strategy has been so successful that I want to market monster repellent. I envision a small spray bottle that sits near the register at children's shops, an impulse item, with a label so fanciful and engaging that it is hard to resist—comic illustrations of monsters with alarmed expressions beautifully drawn in bright ink. The text, a quote from the old Cornish prayer, would readMonster Repellent: for all ghoulies and ghosties and long-legged beasties and things that go bump in the night.

But I am not a mother who can find an entrepreneurial hour away. I am battling a larger monster in our home; a beast out of Goya's last visions is hunkered down in the middle of the living room, its bony spine bumping the ceiling, tongue up the chimney, yellow fingers and horny toes reaching into every room. In the moonlight, huge leathery wings beat against the brick terrace beyond Zack's window. Its demeanor is strangely impassive. It has no grudge against us. It is simply being itself by devouring my child. And I am trying to keep Zack alive long enough for the doctors to find their monster repellent.

In those lavender-scented moments in Zack's room, however, I am triumphant inside my tired blue mommy sweat suit—the uniform that enables me to jump out of bed already dressed and ready for any emergency.

A few days later, Zack and I are sitting on his bed, the bottom bunk. The Brio wooden train set, as always, is spread out on the cork floor. Zack is holding Bumby. I am holding a small, blunt navy sneaker. My son turns to face me, intently silent for a moment, his dark eyes huge. Then he speaks: "Mom, I love you more than trains."

Over the next several months, the right side of Zack's neck and his cheek become increasingly painful and swollen. He is no longer able to turn his head to the right. A new monster has overpowered his weakened immune system. A microscopic one with a large name that we learn later: Mycobacterium avium-intracellulare. From one side he looks perfect, an angelic 5-year-old; from the other, purple and suppurating with infection, grotesque. He knows it. When he puts on his yellow terry Halloween kitty-cat hood that covers the sides of his face, he says, "Now I look the way I used to."

Soon, Zack spends most of his time in the white bunk bed in his room. I keep him at home surrounded by his beloved trains and stuffed animals, will not let him end his life in a strange room in the Formica twilight of a hospital. Nurses come every night. He loves and charms all who care for him. Theresa, one of the favorites, is a kindhearted and zaftig young woman.

"Mom, when I grow up, I'm going to marry Theresa. She would make a good wife."

"Why is that, Zack?"

"Because she has soft breasts."

One day, as I am straightening up Zack's room, Theresa enters for her shift after a week away. She is disturbed by the spread of infection in his swollen face and she asks Zack, who is in his bed against the wall, whether his cheek is bothering him very much. He answers:

"Well, my momma has made me a bandage [to protect it] so now I can lie facing there"—he points to the large window on the opposite wall—"and watch the sun rise." Theresa, speechless, turns toward me with tears in her eyes.

Zack becomes aware of Death's presence. And, not surprisingly, he is preoccupied by ghosts. He fixates on a Ghostbusters toy he sees on TV, and Theresa, a soft touch, brings it for him. The Ghostbuster gun is junky plastic, basically a flashlight that projects cartoons of menacing monsters while making loud tinny machine-gun sounds. He is disappointed. This is scary and ugly.

"Don't worry, I'll fix this for you, Pumpkin," I say, and go out to my studio to see what I can do.

First I disarm the noisemaker. Next, I take apart the card with the transparencies—in frames that rotate around the bulb just like the View-Master of my childhood—and remove the ghoulish pictures. I find some clear Mylar film, Mylar inks, and pen nibs. Then I cut and insert a new plastic circle upon which I have drawn tiny images in the one-inch spaces. I hurry back and give him the toy. Shining on the white wall of his room as he flicks the button are "Betadine Bear," a smiling Thomas the Tank Engine, and Bumby in different poses—standing, sitting, hanging from a pink balloon in the clouds against blue sky, and *I love you. To Zack from Mom* surrounded with hearts.

In his last week, Zack says, "Take me to Dr. Lilliana, Mom. She'll fix me up." I tell him the doctors are looking for the right medicine. He trusts they will find it. But no repellent exists. The monsters are unstoppable.

Days after his memorial service in the backyard, I return to my studio to press bits of old zinc type into a piece of soft wax. Cast in sterling, it becomes a bangle bracelet—a torn strip of silver with small dingbat hearts pressed into an irregular edge and a tiny train disappearing into the overlapping ends—a magic charm to beckon, not repel. Each morning I slip my hand inside my son's words. *I love you more than trains* circles the pulse points of my wrist: a silver incantation that summons a small ghostie.

Things are different now. There is no more Sunday chamber music. The gray-green volume disappeared long ago. In the empty yard, the only ghosts are my memories. I understand why the mother in Andersen's story was unafraid to follow Death down into a grave to find her boy.

I would welcome a haunting.

Anna Belle Kaufman's tragic account of the death of her young son from AIDS opens with Kaufman's memory of her fear of a childhood tale where Death appears to a mother weeping at her child's grave. Kaufman ends her narrative by stating that she now understands the story and no longer fears it. Why?

Kaufman's narrative has a number of recurring themes or symbols—monsters, trains, and the color "grey-green." Choose one of these items and analyze how it relates to the essay as a whole. What does it literally represent? What does it represent symbolically?

Acclaimed black lesbian and poet Audre Lorde used her literary talent to fight against racism, sexism, and homophobia. Her work includes From a Land Where Other People Live *(1973),* The Black Unicorn *(1978), and the American Book Award-winning* A Burst of Life. *The piece below is a speech Lorde first gave at the Modern Language Association meeting in 1977 in which she calls on people to speak out about their own experiences with cancer.*

THE TRANSFORMATION OF SILENCE INTO LANGUAGE AND ACTION

BY AUDRE LORDE

I would like to preface my remarks on the transformation of silence into language and action with a poem. The title of it is "A Song for Many Movements" and this reading is dedicated to Winnie Mandela. Winnie Mandela is a South African freedom fighter who is in exile now somewhere in South Africa. She had been in prison and had been released and was picked up again after she spoke out against the recent jailing of black school children who were singing freedom songs, and who were charged with public violence . . . "A Song for Many Movements":

> Nobody wants to die on the way
> caught between ghosts of whiteness
> and the real water
> none of us wanted to leave
> our bones
> on the way to salvation
> three planets to the left
> a century of light years ago
> our spices are separate and particular
> but our skins sing in complimentary keys
> at a quarter to eight mean time
> we were telling the same stories
> over and over and over.

Broken down gods survive
in the crevasses and mudpots
of every beleaguered city
where it is obvious
there are too many bodies
to cart to the ovens
or gallows
and our uses have become
more important than our silence
after the fall
too many empty cases
of blood to bury or burn
there will be no body left
to listen
and our labor
has become more important
than our silence.

Our labor has become
more important
than our silence.

I have come to believe over and over again that what is most important to me must be spoken, made verbal and shared, even at the risk of having it bruised or misunderstood. That the speaking profits me, beyond any other effect.

I was forced to look upon myself and my living with a harsh and urgent clarity that has left me still shaken but much stronger. Some of what I experienced during that time has helped elucidate for me much of what I feel concerning the transformation of silence into language and action.

In becoming forcibly and essentially aware of my mortality, and of what I wished and wanted for my life, however short it might be, priorities and omissions became strongly etched in a merciless light, and what I most regretted were my silences. Of what had I *ever* been afraid? To question or to speak as I believed could have meant pain, or death. But we all hurt in so many different ways, all the time, and pain will either change, or end. Death, on the other hand, is the final silence. And that might be coming quickly, now, without regard for whether I had ever spoken what needed to be said, or had only betrayed myself into small silences, while I planned someday to speak, or waited for someone else's words.

I was going to die, if not sooner then later, whether or not I had ever spoken myself. My silences had not protected me. Your silence will not protect you.

What are the words you do not yet have? What do you need to say? What are the tyrannies you swallow day by day and attempt to make your own, until you will sicken and die of them, still in silence? Perhaps for some of you here today, I am the face of one of your fears. Because I am woman, because I am black, because I am lesbian, because I am myself, a black woman warrior poet doing my work, come to ask you, are you doing yours?

And, of course, I am afraid—you can hear it in my voice—because the transformation of silence into language and action is an act of self-revelation and that always seems fraught with danger. But my daughter, when I told her of our topic and my difficulty with it, said, "Tell them about how you're never really a whole person if you remain silent, because there's always that one little piece inside you that wants to be spoken out, and if you keep ignoring it, it gets madder and madder and hotter and hotter, and if you don't speak it out one day it will just up and punch you in the mouth."

In the cause of silence, each one of us draws the face of her own fear—fear of contempt, of censure, or some judgment, or recognition, of challenge, of annihilation. But most of all, I think, we fear the very visibility without which we cannot truly live.

And that visibility which makes us most vulnerable is that which also is the source of our greatest strength. Because the machine will try to grind you into dust anyway, whether or not we speak. We can sit in our corners mute forever while our sisters and our selves are wasted, while our children are distorted and destroyed, while our earth is poisoned, we can sit in our safe corners mute as bottles, and we still will be no less afraid.

Each of us is here now because in one way or another we share a commitment to language and to the power of language, and to the reclaiming of that language which has been made to work against us. In the transformation of silence into language and action, it is vitally necessary for each one of us to establish or examine her function in that transformation, and to recognize her role as vital within that transformation.

For those of us who write, it is necessary to scrutinize not only the truth of what we speak, but the truth of that language by which we speak it. For others, it is to share and spread also those words that are meaningful to us. But primarily for us all, it is necessary to teach by living and speaking those truths which we believe and know beyond understanding. Because in this way alone can we survive, by taking part in a process of life that is creative and continuing, that is growth.

And it is never without fear; Of visibility, of the harsh light of scrutiny and perhaps judgment, of pain, of death. But we have lived through all of those already, in silence, except death. And I remind myself all the time now, that if I were to have been born mute, or had maintained an oath of silence my whole life long for safety, I would still have suffered, and I would still die. It is very good for establishing perspective.

We can learn to work and speak when we are afraid in the same way we have learned to work and speak when we are tired. For we have been socialized to respect fear more than our own needs for language and definition, and while we wait in silence for that final luxury of fearlessness, the weight of that silence will choke us.

The fact that we are here and that I speak now these words is an attempt to break that silence and bridge some of those differences between us, for it is not difference which immobilizes us, but silence. And there are so many silences to be broken.

Using your campus or local library, or an Internet search engine, such as Google or Bing, find examples of Audre Lorde's poetry. Do any of her other poems speak to the theme of death? Does her poetry reflect, in your opinion, the kind of feminist concerns she raises in her above speech?

Upon learning she may die of cancer, Lorde speaks about the things she cares most about—helping women find the courage to speak up publicly about issues that matter to them. If you were facing the possibility of death, what issue or issues would you most want to bring to public awareness? Write a short essay—3 to 5 paragraphs—about an issue you value, but may be afraid to speak about publicly.

Roman Catholic religious sister Helen Prejean is a member of the Congregation of St. Joseph and is a well-known American advocate for the international abolishment of the death penalty. She began her prison ministry in 1981 in the Louisiana State Penitentiary, which inspired her 1993 book, Dead Man Walking. The book spent 31 weeks on the New York Times Best-Seller list, and was made into a major motion picture starring Susan Sarandon and Sean Penn. In the excerpt below, Prejean narrates her account of the execution of convicted murderer Patrick Sonnier.

excerpt from

DEAD MAN WALKING

By Helen Prejean, C.S.J.

"Just a little more coffee," Pat says.

"That's the shrink," he whispers.

The telephone rings again. Heart-stop. Wait. See if Rabelais comes with news. I imagine the words that will make all the difference: "Sonnier, you got a stay."

I look at my watch: 5:15. I call Joe Nursey again.

"Any word from Millard?"

"He's still at the mansion," Joe says. "All he said was that he was going to stay there until everything is all right."

What can that mean, I wonder. Why is he there so long? It must not have gone well. If it had, Millard would be calling us.

There is a gush of air as the front door opens. Pat looks. "It's Wardens Maggio and Thomas," he says. I turn to look at them. They are wearing three-piece suits. Each has a shortwave radio at his side.

It is 6:00. The sun has set behind the trees. Afternoon has now turned to evening. The sparrows are silent, nested up under the eaves for the night. It is time for Pat's final meal.

Pat tells me what he has ordered: a steak, medium-well-done, potato salad, green beans, hot rolls with butter, a green salad, a Coke, and apple pie for dessert.

Warden Maggio comes to the door to tell Pat that the chef has been giving "real special attention" to his meal and will be bringing it in shortly. He is to eat it inside his cell so that his hands can be freed of the handcuffs and Maggio is granting special permission for me to join Pat inside the tier just outside his cell, where I will be served my tray.

The fluorescent lights are on now in the building. You can see the light shining on the polished tiles. I think of how comforting the orange glow of a lamp is in a window, when you come home in the evening and the darkness is closing in. But these lights are cold and greenish white. I am waiting for the telephone to ring.

It does. Just as the chef brings Pat his meal and I am served mine. I look up through the metal door and see Captain Rabelais's face. He is looking at me and shaking his head no. Warden Maggio tells Pat in a matter-of-fact voice: "Sonnier, the Fifth Circuit turned you down."

I do not give any outward sign, but inside I fall headlong down a chasm. *The Fifth Circuit turned him down.* Only Millard left now, with the governor.

Pat teases the warden. "Well, Warden, I won the last round"—in August—"and it looks like you're winning this one." He waves his spoon in the air and then points it toward his heaping plate and laughs. "At least I got me this good meal off you, and I'm sure going to enjoy every bit of it."

And I am remembering his words: "They are not going to break me." I look down at my own tray of food and know that I will not be eating one bite. There is a glass of iced tea and I sip that. I feel unreal.

Pat talks and eats and talks. He is like a man in a bar who tells stories too loudly. The telephone rings again. It's Rabelais at the door. "Sonnier, the U.S. Supreme Court turned you down."

Millard. Still no word from him.

It is dark outside.

Pat has eaten everything on his plate except some of the green salad. He eats the apple pie, then lays the spoon on the tray and says, "There, finished, and I wasn't even hungry."

Warden Maggio comes to the tier just outside Pat's cell. Pat says to him, "Warden, tell that chef, tell him for me that he did a really great job. The steak was perfect,"—he makes a circle with his thumb and forefinger—"and the potato salad, and really great apple pie."

The warden assures him he will pass on his compliments to the chef. "He put himself out for you, Sonnier, he really did."

"And you tell him, Warden," Pat says again, "that I am truly, truly appreciative."

I rise from my chair and hand my tray of untouched food to Rabelais. The guards are changing shifts. I look at the face of the guard leaving the tier. Is he finished for the night? Will he be going home to his family now? Will his children ask him questions? His face is tight. I cannot tell what he is thinking.

I give Pat some moments alone in his cell. I tell him I'm going to the rest room. The building is buzzing now. Guards are everywhere, and men in three-piece suits. A secretary has arrived and has begun typing. You can hear the *click, click, click* of the typewriter. It sounds like a business office.

"What's she typing?" I whisper to Rabelais.

"Forms for the witnesses to sign," he says.

The large aluminum coffee pot is percolating a fresh batch of coffee. I see that someone has put a white tablecloth on a table and has placed ballpoint pens in the center of the table.

I go into the rest room. A few precious moments of privacy. I look at the sparkling tiled walls, the clean white fixtures, ample soap, paper towels. Everything is so clean. I keep feeling as if I'm in a hospital, the cleanliness, attendants following a protocol . . . *Oh, God, help me, help me, please*, and I harness all my energies, I gather myself inside like someone who pulls her coat tight around her in a strong wind.

I leave the rest room and glance down at the path of tiles that leads to the white metal door at the end of the room. Rabelais comes through that door now with someone in jeans and a plaid shirt and jacket. Must be the electrician. Rabelais locks the door behind him.

I go back to the visitor door. Pat is still in his cell. The phone rings on the wall near the cell. The guard on the tier walks down and answers it and hands the phone to Pat. I can see the coiled wire of the phone along the wall until it disappears into the cell. I can hear Pat's voice rising and falling. "Thank you, Mr. Millard, thank you for what you and all the others done for me. I got you too late. If I had had you sooner . . ." Silence. "No, Mr. Millard, no you didn't fail, you didn't fail, it's the justice system in this country, it stinks. It stinks bad, Mr. Millard, no, no, no, Mr. Millard, you didn't fail . . ."

And now for the first time I know surely that he's going to die. I look at my watch. It is 8:40.

I go to Captain Rabelais and ask to make a couple of phone calls. I call the Sisters to ask them to pray, and I call my mother to let her know I am okay and to ask her to pray.

I go back to the visitor door. The guard inside is putting the shackles on Pat's hands and feet inside the cell. He opens the cell door and Pat comes over to the metal folding chair by the door. As he approaches the chair his legs sag and he drops to one knee beside the chair. He looks up at me. "Sister Helen, I'm going to die."

My soul rushes toward him. I am standing with my hands against the mesh screen, as close as I can get to him. I pray and ask God to comfort him, cushion him, wrap him round, give him courage to face death, to step across the river, to die with love. The words are pouring from me.

His moment of weakness has passed. He sits in the metal chair and calls to Rabelais for a cup of coffee. He notices as he pulls a cigarette from the pack in his shirt pocket that there are just a few left. "Ought to just about make it," he says.

He makes out his will, one single line on a piece of yellow legal paper. "I give to Sister Helen Prejean all my possessions." Rabelais has someone notarize the will.

That done, Pat composes a letter to Eddie.

"Dear Brother," he says, "don't worry about me, I'll be okay. You keep your cool, it's the only way you'll make it in this place. When you get out someday, take care of Mama. Remember the promise you made to me. I love you. Your big brother."

The front door is opening regularly now. Pat looks up every time he hears someone coming in. He watches. He notices everything.

A guard called Slick comes through the front door. He is a big, burly man with a shiny bald head and he is carrying a small canvas bag. Rabelais comes and asks me to step out into the foyer. Slick, accompanied by two other guards, goes into the cell with Pat. I quietly walk up and down the foyer. I look down at my black leather pumps. I walk back and forth, back and forth. "Please, God, help him, please help him."

A chaplain named Penton approaches me. He is dressed in a bright green suit. I have the feeling that he has worked here for a long time. He tells me that he is here "in case the inmate might need my services at this time." Then he tells me to prepare myself for the "visual shock" of Pat's shaved head. "They must remove the hair to reduce the possibility of its catching fire," he says. I keep walking slowly up and down the foyer and he walks alongside me. I am thinking of Gandhi. I am thinking of Camus. "Resist, do not collaborate in any way with a deed which you believe is evil . . . resist . . ." In his *Reflections* Camus tells of a Russian man about to be hanged by the Tsar's executioners who repulsed the priest who came forward to offer a blessing: *"Go away and commit no sacrilege."* (p. 224)

Camus says about Christians:

> *The unbeliever cannot keep from thinking that men who have set at the center of their faith the staggering victim of a judicial error ought at least to hesitate before committing legal murder. Believers might also be reminded that Emperor Julian, before his conversion, did not want to give official offices to Christians because they systematically refused to pronounce death sentences or to have anything to do with them. For five centuries Christians therefore believed that the strict moral teaching of their master forbade killing. (p. 224)*

I talk to Penton about a phone call I received from one of the Catholic prison chaplains several weeks ago. The priest had asked me which funeral home would pick up Pat's body if the execution were to take place. Before I got this call, Pat had told me that the old priest had approached him in his cell and said brightly, attempting humor, "Well, Sonnier, what are we gonna do with the body?" Pat had said angrily, "Don't you call my mama and ask her that. Don't you dare upset her. Call Sister Helen." And so the phone call had come to me, and I had said I had no idea who would pick up the body.

I see how easy it is for chaplains, on the payroll, to play their part in this "uncontrollable but necessary business," and I ask whether it should be the role of the chaplain to collaborate with the prison in planning the "disposal of the remains" of the person the state has killed. Penton tells me he will think about that. (He does. Later he sees to it that chaplains no longer make burial arrangements for executed prisoners.)

Rabelais comes to tell me that I can go back now to Pat.

I move to my side of the visitor door and wait for Pat to come from the cell.

Slick and crew are just coming through the door from the tier. One of the guards is carrying a towel and small broom, another a brown paper bag with Pat's curly black hair in it. Slick is zipping up his canvas shaving kit. He moves quickly. I look at Pat as he comes back to the metal chair. His head looks whitish gray and shiny. His hair is gone now, eyebrows too. He looks like a bird without feathers. I see that they have also cut his left pants leg off at the knee. "They shaved the calf of my leg," he says, and he holds out his leg for me to see. I see a tattooed number.

"What's that number?" I ask.

"That's from when I was at Angola before," he tells me. "In case anybody killed me, I wanted them to be able to identify my body."

I notice that he is wearing a clean white T-shirt.

I look at my watch and Pat looks at his. It is 10:30. Everything is ready now. All Pat needs to do now is die. He asks the guard for a pen and writes in his Bible, up in the front, where there is a special place for family history—births, marriages, deaths.

"There," he says, " I wrote it in my own hand."

The guard unlocks the door and hands me the Bible. I look at the front page. He has written loving words to me, words of thanks. Then I see under "Deaths" his name and the date, April 4, 1984.

I remember Jesus' words that we do not know the day nor the hour. But Pat knows. And in knowing he dies and then dies again.

Two guards inside the tier stand on stepladders and hang black curtains over the windows along the top.

"They don't want other inmates to see the lights dim when the switch is pulled," Pat tells me. He is smoking and talking now, his talk a torrent, a flood, all coming together now, snatches from childhood and teasing Eddie and school and the sugar-cane fields gleaming in the sun and Star, what will happen to her, and his Mama, to please see about his Mama, and Eddie, will he be able to keep his cool in this place, and if only he knew when the current first hit that he would die right away . . .

He begins to shiver. "It's cold in here," he says, and the guard gets a blue denim shirt from the cell and puts it around his shoulders, then goes back to his position at the end of the tier.

People are chatting nervously in the foyer and lobby now. The witnesses must all be inside by now, the press, all the prison officials. You can hear the hum of talk and some snatches of conversation. You can hear when someone inserts coins into one of the drink machines and the clunk of the can when it comes out.

I look around. There, standing behind me, are Bill Quigley and Millard Farmer. I rise and move toward them and have to hold myself in close check. Their presence, their love, knowing they have tried so hard to save Pat's life, makes me want to weep. But no tears now. Bill gives my hand a tight squeeze. Millard does not look into my eyes. We move to the visitor door. Guards bring two chairs for Millard and Bill. What words to say during these (I look at my watch) last fifty minutes? Pat says, "Look at the time, it's flying."

The old priest approaches us. I rise and go over to him, "Let Elmo know"—Pat hates being called Elmo—"I'm available for the last sacraments," he tells me.

I give his message to Pat.

Pat shakes his head. "No, I don't like that man. All of you, my friends who love me, you make me feel close to God. Sister Helen, when it is all over, you receive communion for both of us."

I promise that I will.

The warden approaches Millard and asks him to step into the foyer. In a few moments Millard comes back. "Pat, the governor has given permission for me to be a witness."

Thank God. It strengthens me to know that Millard will be there too.

Captain Rabelais asks the three of us to step into the foyer for a moment. Three guards go into the cell with Pat. It is 11:30. No one can say much, but Bill whispers to me that Ann, Lory, and Kathleen and some other Sisters are at the front gate.

People are all still milling around in the large room. The witnesses have not been seated yet. Mr. LeBlanc and Mr. Bourque must be here. What are they going through? Will this help heal their loss? I wonder. I hear the toilet flush in Pat's cell.

Rabelais summons us back to the door. Pat comes from his cell, his legs and hands cuffed. Anger flickers in his eyes. "A grown man, and I have to leave this world with a diaper on," he says.

"I'll be free of all this," he says, shaking his handcuffs. "No more cells, no more bars, no more life in a cage," he says.

He reaches in his pocket for a cigarette. He turns and shows the guard, "Look, the last one. It'll see me out."

Warden Maggio approaches us. He is flanked by six or seven very large guards. It must be midnight. "Time to go, Sonnier," Maggio says. One of the guards takes Bill out to the foyer, and another tells Millard to follow him. I stand to the side of the door. I will walk with Pat. I am holding his Bible. I have selected the Isaiah passage to read as we walk, the words that were in the song, words that Pat has heard and the words will be there for him to hear again, if he can hear words at all, when he will be trying to put one foot in front of another, walking from here to there across these polished tiles.

"Warden," he asks, "can I ask one favor? Can Sister Helen touch my arm?"

The Warden nods his head.

I am standing behind him. Guards, a mountain of blue, surround us. I put my hand on his shoulder. He is tall. I can barely reach. It is the first time I have ever touched him.

We walk. Pat walks and the chains scrape across the floor. God has heard his prayer. His legs are holding up, he is walking.

I read Isaiah's words:

> Do not be afraid . . . I have called you by
> your name, you are mine.
> Should you pass through the sea,
> I will be with you . . .
> Should you walk through the fire,
> you will not be scorched,
> and the flames will not burn you."
>
> (43:2)

As we pass through the lobby the old priest raises his hand in blessing.

We stop. There is the oak chair, dark and gleaming in the bright fluorescent lights. There are the witnesses all seated behind a Plexiglas window. There is a big clock on the wall behind the chair. There is an exhaust fan, already turned on to get rid of the smell of burning flesh. Two guards have firmly taken hold of my arms and are moving me toward the witness room. I lean toward Pat and kiss him on the back.

"Pat, pray for me."

He turns around toward me and says, his voice husky and eager like a young boy's, "I will, Sister Helen, I will."

I see Millard then and I sit in the chair beside him. He reaches over and takes my hand. Mr. Bourque and Mr. LeBlanc are seated on the first row over to the right of us. Their faces are expressionless.

There is a small podium with a microphone on it and Pat is standing behind it. I can see past him to a wall of green painted plywood with a slit of a window behind which the executioner waits.

The warden is standing over in the right-hand corner next to a red telephone.

"Have any last words, Sonnier?" he asks.

"Yes, sir, I do," Pat says, and he looks at the two fathers, but addresses his words to only one of them. "Mr. LeBlanc, I don't want to leave this world with any hatred in my heart. I want to ask your forgiveness for what me and Eddie done, but Eddie done it." Mr. LeBlanc nods his head. Mr. Bourque turns to Mr. LeBlanc and asks, "What about me?"

Pat is in the chair now and guards are moving quickly, removing the leg irons and handcuffs and replacing them with the leather straps. One guard has removed his left shoe. They are strapping his trunk, his legs, his arms. He finds my face. He says, "I love you." I stretch my hand toward him. "I love you, too."

He attempts a smile (he told me he would try to smile) but manages only to twitch.

A metal cap is placed on his head and an electrode is screwed in at the top and connected to a wire that comes from a box behind the chair. An electrode is fastened to his leg. A strap placed around his chin holds his head tightly against the back of the chair. He grimaces. He cannot speak anymore. A grayish green cloth is placed over his face.

Millard says, "Father forgive them, for they know not what they do."

Only the warden remains in the room now, only the warden and the man strapped into the chair. The red telephone is silent. I close my eyes and do not see as the warden nods his head, the signal to the executioner to do his work.

Why, in your opinion, did Helen Prejean write *Dead Man Walking*? Do you think it matters to her if Pat Sonnier is guilty or innocent? Explain.

Working together in groups, using the resources of your campus library and/or the Internet, find out which states have banned (or are working to ban) the death penalty and which continue to use it. In each case, what reasons do states give for their choice?

Using the electronic resources of your campus or local library, access the publication *CQ Researcher* and find the November 2011 article titled "Death Penalty Debates: Is the Capital Punishment System Working?" by Kenneth Jost. What reasons does the article give for why the system is not working? What reasons does it provide for why it is working?

Helen Prejean is an advocate for the abolishment of the death penalty in the United States. What was your response to her account of Pat Sonnier's execution? What do you think about the issue as a whole? In a page or two, write a letter to Helen Prejean outlining your responses to both the excerpt you read from her book, as well as to the issue itself.

Best known for his 1952 children's novel Charlotte's Web, *E. B. White wrote for both* The New Yorker *and* Harper's *magazines from the late 1920s until just prior to his death in 1985. The piece below first appeared in* Harper's *magazine in 1941 and is considered by critics to be one of his finest essays.*

ONCE MORE TO THE LAKE

By E. B. White

One summer, along about 1904, my father rented a camp on a lake in Maine and took us all there for the month of August. We all got ringworm from some kittens and had to rub Pond's Extract on our arms and legs night and morning, and my father rolled over in a canoe with all his clothes on; but outside of that the vacation was a success and from then on none of us ever thought there was any place in the world like that lake in Maine. We returned summer after summer—always on August 1st for one month. I have since become a salt-water man, but sometimes in summer there are days when the restlessness of the tides and the fearful cold of the sea water and the incessant wind which blows across the afternoon and into the evening make me wish for the placidity of a lake in the woods. A few weeks ago this feeling got so strong I bought myself a couple of bass hooks and a spinner and returned to the lake where we used to go, for a week's fishing and to revisit old haunts.

I took along my son, who had never had any fresh water up his nose and who had seen lily pads only from train windows. On the journey over to the lake I began to wonder what it would be like. I wondered how time would have marred this unique, this holy spot—the coves and streams, the hills that the sun set behind, the camps and the paths behind the camps. I was sure that the tarred road would have found it out and I wondered in what other ways it would be desolated. It is strange how much you can remember about places like that once you allow your mind to return into the grooves which lead back. You remember one thing, and that suddenly reminds you of another thing. I guess I remembered clearest of all the early mornings, when the lake was cool and motionless, remembered how the bedroom smelled of the lumber it was made of and of the wet woods whose scent entered through the screen. The partitions in the camp were thin and did not extend clear to the top of the rooms, and as I was always the first up I would dress softly so as not to wake the others, and sneak out into the sweet outdoors and start out in the canoe, keeping close along the shore in the long shadows of the pines. I remembered being very careful never to rub my paddle against the gunwale for fear of disturbing the stillness of the cathedral.

The lake had never been what you would call a wild lake. There were cottages sprinkled around the shores, and it was in farming although the shores of the lake were quite heavily wooded. Some of the cottages were owned by nearby farmers, and you would live at the shore and eat your meals at the farmhouse. That's what our family did. But although it wasn't wild, it was a fairly large and undisturbed lake and there were places in it which, to a child at least, seemed infinitely remote and primeval.

I was right about the tar: it led to within half a mile of the shore. But when I got back there, with my boy, and we settled into a camp near a farmhouse and into the kind of summertime I had known, I could tell that it was going to be pretty much the same as it had been before—I knew it, lying in bed the first morning, smelling the bedroom, and hearing the boy sneak quietly out and go off along the shore in a boat. I began to sustain the illusion that he was I, and therefore, by simple transposition, that I was my father. This sensation persisted, kept cropping up all the time we were there. It was not an entirely new feeling, but in this setting it grew much stronger. I seemed to be living a dual existence. I would be in the middle of some simple act, I would be picking up a bait box or laying down a table fork, or I would be saying something, and suddenly it would be not I but my father who was saying the words or making the gesture. It gave me a creepy sensation.

We went fishing the first morning. I felt the same damp moss covering the worms in the bait can, and saw the dragonfly alight on the tip of my rod as it hovered a few inches from the surface of the water. It was the arrival of this fly that convinced me beyond any doubt that everything was as it always had been, that the years were a mirage and there had been no years. The small waves were the same, chucking the rowboat under the chin as we fished at anchor, and the boat was the same boat, the same color green and the ribs broken in the same places, and under the floor-boards the same freshwater leavings and debris—the dead helgramite, the wisps of moss, the rusty discarded fishhook, the dried blood from yesterday's catch. We stared silently at the tips of our rods, at the dragonflies that came and went. I lowered the tip of mine into the water, tentatively, pensively dislodging the fly, which darted two feet away, poised, darted two feet back, and came to rest again a little farther up the rod. There had been no years between the ducking of this dragonfly and the other one—the one that was part of memory. I looked at the boy, who was silently watching his fly, and it was my hands that held his rod, my eyes watching. I felt dizzy and didn't know which rod I was at the end of.

We caught two bass, hauling them in briskly as though they were mackerel, pulling them over the side of the boat in a businesslike manner without any landing net, and stunning them with a blow on the back of the head. When we got back for a swim before lunch, the lake was exactly where we had left it, the same number of inches from the dock, and there was only the merest suggestion of a breeze. This seemed an utterly enchanted sea, this lake you could leave to its own devices for a few hours and come back to, and find that it had not stirred, this constant and trustworthy body of water. In the shallows, the dark, water-soaked sticks and twigs, smooth and old, were undulating in clusters on the bottom against the clean ribbed sand, and the track of the mussel was plain. A school of minnows swam by, each minnow with its small, individual shadow, doubling the attendance, so clear and sharp in the sunlight. Some of the other campers were in swimming, along the shore, one of them with a cake of soap, and the water felt thin and clear and insubstantial. Over the years there had been this person with the cake of soap, this cultist, and here he was. There had been no years.

Up to the farmhouse to dinner through the teeming, dusty field, the road under our sneakers was only a two-track road. The middle track was missing, the one with the marks of the hooves and the splotches of dried, flaky manure. There had always been three tracks to choose from in choosing which track to walk in; now the choice was narrowed down to two. For a moment I missed terribly the middle alternative. But the way led past the tennis court, and something about the way it lay there in the sun reassured me; the tape had loosened along the backline, the alleys were green with plantains and other weeds, and the net (installed in June and removed in September) sagged in the dry noon, and the whole place steamed with midday heat and hunger and emptiness. There was a choice of pie for dessert, and one was blueberry and one was apple, and the waitresses were the same country girls, there having been no passage of time, only the illusion of it as in a dropped curtain—the waitresses were still fifteen; their hair had been washed, that was the only difference—they had been to the movies and seen the pretty girls with the clean hair.

Summertime, oh summertime, pattern of life indelible, the fade proof lake, the woods unshatterable, the pasture with the sweet fern and the juniper forever and ever, summer without end; this was the background, and the life along the shore was the design, the cottages with their innocent and tranquil design, their tiny docks with the flagpole and the American flag floating against the white clouds in the blue sky, the little paths over the roots of the trees leading from camp to camp and the paths leading back to the outhouses and the can of lime for sprinkling, and at the souvenir counters at the store the miniature birch-bark canoes and the post cards that showed things looking a little better than they looked. This was the American family at play, escaping the city heat, wondering whether the newcomers at the camp at the head of the cove were "common" or "nice," wondering whether it was true that the people who drove up for Sunday dinner at the farmhouse were turned away because there wasn't enough chicken.

It seemed to me, as I kept remembering all this, that those times and those summers had been infinitely precious and worth saving. There had been jollity and peace and goodness. The arriving (at the beginning of August) had been so big a business in itself, at the railway station the farm wagon drawn up, the first smell of the pine-laden air, the first glimpse of the smiling farmer, and the great importance of the trunks and your father's enormous authority in such matters, and the feel of the wagon under you for the long ten-mile haul, and at the top of the last long hill catching the first view of the lake after eleven months of not seeing this cherished body of water. The shouts and cries of the other campers when they saw you, and the trunks to be unpacked, to give up their rich burden. (Arriving was less exciting nowadays, when you sneaked up in your car and parked it under a tree near the camp and took out the bags and in five minutes it was all over, no fuss, no loud wonderful fuss about trunks.)

Peace and goodness and jollity. The only thing that was wrong now, really, was the sound of the place, an unfamiliar nervous sound of the outboard motors. This was the note that jarred, the one thing that would sometimes break the illusion and set the years moving. In those other summertimes, all motors were inboard; and when they were at a little distance, the noise they made was a sedative, an ingredient of summer sleep. They were one-cylinder and two-cylinder engines, and some were make-and-break and some were jump-spark, but they all made a sleepy sound across the lake. The one-lungers throbbed and fluttered, and the twin-cylinder ones purred and purred, and that was a quiet sound too. But now the campers all had outboards. In the daytime, in the hot mornings, these motors made a petulant, irritable sound; at night, in the still evening when the afterglow lit the water, they whined about one's ears like mosquitoes. My boy loved our rented outboard, and his great desire was to achieve single-handed mastery over it, and authority, and he soon learned the trick of choking it a little (but not too much), and the adjustment of the needle valve. Watching him I would remember the things you could do with the old one-cylinder engine with the heavy flywheel, how you could have it eating out of your hand if you got really close to it spiritually. Motor boats in those days didn't have clutches, and you would make a landing by shutting off the motor at the proper time and coasting in with a dead rudder. But there was a way of reversing them, if you learned the trick, by cutting the switch and putting it on again exactly on the final dying revolution of the flywheel, so that it would kick back against compression and begin reversing. Approaching a dock in a strong following breeze, it was difficult to slow up sufficiently by the ordinary coasting method, and if a boy felt he had complete mastery over his motor, he was tempted to keep it running beyond its time and then reverse it a few feet from the dock. It took a cool nerve, because if you threw the switch a twentieth of a second too soon you would catch the flywheel when it still had speed enough to go up past center, and the boat would leap ahead, charging bull-fashion at the dock.

We had a good week at the camp. The bass were biting well and the sun shone endlessly, day after day. We would be tired at night and lie down in the accumulated heat of the little bedrooms after the long hot day and the breeze would stir almost imperceptibly outside and the smell of the swamp drift in through the rusty screens. Sleep would come easily and in the morning the red squirrel would be on the roof, tapping out his gay routine. I kept remembering everything, lying in bed in the mornings—the small steamboat that had a long rounded stern like the lip of a Ubangi, and how quietly she ran on the moonlight sails, when the older boys played their mandolins and the girls sang and we ate doughnuts dipped in sugar, and how sweet the music was on the water in the shining night, and what it had felt like to think about girls then.

After breakfast we would go up to the store and the things were in the same place—the minnows in a bottle, the plugs and spinners disarranged and pawed over by the youngsters from the boys' camp, the fig newtons and the Beeman's gum. Outside, the road was tarred and cars stood in front of the store. Inside, all was just as it had always been, except there was more Coca Cola and not so much Moxie and root beer and birch beer and sarsaparilla. We would walk out with a bottle of pop apiece and sometimes the pop would backfire up our noses and hurt. We explored the streams, quietly, where the turtles slid off the sunny logs and dug their way into the soft bottom; and we lay on the town wharf and fed worms to the tame bass. Everywhere we went I had trouble making out which was I, the one walking at my side, the one walking in my pants.

One afternoon while we were there at that lake a thunderstorm came up. It was like the revival of an old melodrama that I had seen long ago with childish awe. The second-act climax of the drama of the electrical disturbance over a lake in America had not changed in any important respect. This was the big scene, still the big scene. The whole thing was so familiar, the first feeling of oppression and heat and a general air around camp of not wanting to go very far away. In mid-afternoon (it was all the same) a curious darkening of the sky, and a lull in everything that had made life tick; and then the way the boats suddenly swung the other way at their moorings with the coming of a breeze out of the new quarter, and the premonitory rumble. Then the kettle drum, then the snare, then the bass drum and cymbals, then crackling light against the dark, and the gods grinning and licking their chops in the hills. Afterward the calm, the rain steadily rustling in the calm lake, the return of light and hope and spirits, and the campers running out in joy and relief to go swimming in the rain, their bright cries perpetuating the deathless joke about how they were getting simply drenched, and the children screaming with delight at the new sensation of bathing in the rain, and the joke about getting drenched linking the generations in a strong indestructible chain. And the comedian who waded in carrying an umbrella.

When the others went swimming my son said he was going in too. He pulled his dripping trunks from the line where they had hung all through the shower, and wrung them out. Languidly, and with no thought of going in, I watched him, his hard little body, skinny and bare, saw him wince slightly as he pulled up around his vitals the small, soggy, icy garment. As he buckled the swollen belt suddenly my groin felt the chill of death.

E. B. White's famous piece about summer and vacationing at the lake does not seem to be about the topic of this book, until the last sentence of the essay: "As he buckled the swollen belt suddenly my groin felt the chill of death." Why is White suddenly reminded of death when he watches his son put on his swimming trunks?

Using the resources of your campus library and/or the Internet, find one or two critiques or reviews of White's essay. What do the authors say about it? Is death mentioned in these evaluations of White's work?

In "Once More to the Lake," the lake itself becomes another character in the essay. How does White personify the lake? What specific words does he use to describe and refer to the lake? What do you think it represents for him?

DEATH

The world is the lucky beneficiary when two such acclaimed writers as Virginia Woolf and Annie Dillard choose the same subject—the death of an ordinary moth—to exercise their considerable literary talents. Woolf's essay, published in 1942—a year after her death by suicide—pairs nicely with Dillard's later piece, which first appeared in Harper's magazine in 1976. While both essays narrate the writer's observation of the natural death of a moth, the two essays vary in terms of how this death affects the writer.

THE DEATH OF THE MOTH

By Virginia Woolf

Moths that fly by day are not properly to be called moths; they do not excite that pleasant sense of dark autumn nights and ivy-blossom which the commonest yellow-underwing asleep in the shadow of the curtain never fails to rouse in us. They are hybrid creatures, neither gay like butterflies nor somber like their own species. Nevertheless the present specimen, with his narrow hay-colored wings, fringed with a tassel of the same color, seemed to be content with life. It was a pleasant morning, mid-September, mild, benignant, yet with a keener breath than that of the summer months. The plough was already scoring the field opposite the window, and where the share had been, the earth was pressed flat and gleamed with moisture. Such vigor came rolling in from the fields and the down beyond that it was difficult to keep the eyes strictly turned upon the book. The rooks too were keeping one of their annual festivities; soaring round the tree tops until it looked as if a vast net with thousands of black knots in it had been cast up into the air; which, after a few moments sank slowly down upon the trees until every twig seemed to have a knot at the end of it. Then, suddenly, the net would be thrown into the air again in a wider circle this time, with the utmost clamor and vociferation, as though to be thrown into the air and settle slowly down upon the tree tops were a tremendously exciting experience.

The same energy which inspired the rooks, the ploughmen, the horses, and even, it seemed, the lean bare-backed downs, sent the moth fluttering from side to side of his square of the windowpane. One could not help watching him.

One, was, indeed, conscious of a queer feeling of pity for him. The possibilities of pleasure seemed that morning so enormous and so various that to have only a moth's part in life, and a day moth's at that, appeared a hard fate, and his zest in enjoying his meager opportunities to the full, pathetic. He flew vigorously to one corner of his compartment, and, after waiting there a second, flew across to the other. What remained for him but to fly to a third corner and then to a fourth? That was all he could do, in spite of the size of the downs, the width of the sky, the far-off smoke of houses, and the romantic voice, now and then, of a steamer out at sea. What he could do he did. Watching him, it seemed as if a fibre, very thin but pure, of the enormous energy of the world had been thrust into his frail and diminutive body. As often as he crossed the pane, I could fancy that a thread of vital light became visible. He was little or nothing but life.

Yet, because he was so small, and so simple a form of the energy that was rolling in at the open window and driving its way through so many narrow and intricate corridors in my own brain and in those of other human beings, there was something marvelous as well as pathetic about him. It was as if someone had taken a tiny bead of pure life and decking it as lightly as possible with down and feathers, had set it dancing and zig-zagging to show us the true nature of life. Thus displayed one could not get over the strangeness of it. One is apt to forget all about life, seeing it humped and bossed and garnished and cumbered so that it has to move with the greatest circumspection and dignity. Again, the thought of all that life might have been had he been born in any other shape caused one to view his simple activities with a kind of pity.

After a time, tired by his dancing apparently, he settled on the window ledge in the sun, and, the queer spectacle being at an end, I forgot about him. Then, looking up, my eye was caught by him. He was trying to resume his dancing, but seemed either so stiff or so awkward that he could only flutter to the bottom of the windowpane; and when he tried to fly across it he failed. Being intent on other matters I watched these futile attempts for a time without thinking, unconsciously waiting for him to resume his flight, as one waits for a machine, that has stopped momentarily, to start again without considering the reason of its failure. After perhaps a seventh attempt he slipped from the wooden ledge and fell, fluttering his wings, on to his back on the window sill. The helplessness of his attitude roused me. It flashed upon me that he was in difficulties; he could no longer raise himself; his legs struggled vainly. But, as

I stretched out a pencil, meaning to help him to right himself, it came over me that the failure and awkwardness were the approach of death. I laid the pencil down again.

The legs agitated themselves once more. I looked as if for the enemy against which he struggled. I looked out of doors. What had happened there? Presumably it was midday, and work in the fields had stopped. Stillness and quiet had replaced the previous animation. The birds had taken themselves off to feed in the brooks. The horses stood still. Yet the power was there all the same, massed outside indifferent, impersonal, not attending to anything in particular. Somehow it was opposed to the little hay-colored moth. It was useless to try to do anything. One could only watch the extraordinary efforts made by those tiny legs against an oncoming doom which could, had it chosen, have submerged an entire city, not merely a city, but masses of human beings; nothing, I knew, had any chance against death. Nevertheless after a pause of exhaustion the legs fluttered again. It was superb this last protest, and so frantic that he succeeded at last in righting himself. One's sympathies, of course, were all on the side of life. Also, when there was nobody to care or to know, this gigantic effort on the part of an insignificant little moth, against a power of such magnitude, to retain what no one else valued or desired to keep, moved one strangely. Again, somehow, one saw life, a pure bead. I lifted the pencil again, useless though I knew it to be. But even as I did so, the unmistakable tokens of death showed themselves. The body relaxed, and instantly grew stiff. The struggle was over. The insignificant little creature now knew death. As I looked at the dead moth, this minute wayside triumph of so great a force over so mean an antagonist filled me with wonder. Just as life had been strange a few minutes before, so death was now as strange. The moth having righted himself now lay most decently and uncomplainingly composed. O yes, he seemed to say, death is stronger than I am.

DEATH

THE DEATH OF A MOTH

By Annie Dillard

TRANSFIGURATION IN A CANDLE FLAME

I live alone with two cats, who sleep on my legs. There is a yellow one, and a black one whose name is Small. In the morning I joke to the black one, Do you remember last night? Do you remember? I throw them both out before breakfast, so I can eat.

There is a spider, too, in the bathroom, of uncertain lineage, bulbous at the abdomen and drab, whose six-inch mess of web works, works somehow, works miraculously, to keep her alive and me amazed. The web is in a corner behind the toilet, connecting tile wall to tile wall. The house is new, the bathroom immaculate, save for the spider, her web, and the sixteen or so corpses she's tossed to the floor.

The corpses appear to be mostly sow bugs, those little armadillo creatures who live to travel flat out in houses, and die round. In addition to sow-bug husks, hollow and sipped empty of color, there are what seem to be two or three wingless moth bodies, one new flake of earwig, and three spider carcasses crinkled and clenched.

I wonder on what fool's errand an earwig, or a moth, or a sow bug, would visit that clean corner of the house behind the toilet; I have not noticed any blind parades of sow bugs blundering into corners. Yet they do hazard there, at a rate of more than one a week, and the spider thrives. Yesterday she was working on the earwig, mouth on gut; today he's on the floor. It must take a certain genius to throw things away from there, to find a straight line through that sticky tangle to the floor.

Today the earwig shines darkly, and gleams, what there is of him: a dorsal curve of thorax and abdomen, and a smooth pair of pincers by which I knew his name. Next week, if the other bodies are any indication, he'll be shrunk and gray, webbed to the floor with dust. The sow bugs beside him are curled and empty, fragile, a breath away from brittle fluff. The spiders lie on their sides, translucent and ragged, their legs drying in knots. The moths stagger against each other, headless, in a confusion of arcing strips of chitin like peeling varnish, like a jumble of buttresses for cathedral vaults, like nothing resembling moths, so that I would hesitate to call them moths, except that I have had some experience with the figure Moth reduced to a nub.

Two summers ago I was camped alone in the Blue Ridge Mountains of Virginia. I had hauled myself and gear up there to read, among other things, *The Day on Fire*, by James Ullman, a novel about Rimbaud that had made me want to be a writer when I was sixteen; I was hoping it would do it again. So I read every day sitting under a tree by my tent, while warblers sang in the leaves overhead and bristle worms trailed their inches over the twiggy dirt at my feet; and I read every night by candlelight, while barred owls called in the forest and pale moths seeking mates massed round my head in the clearing, where my light made a ring.

Moths kept flying into the candle. They would hiss and recoil, reeling upside down in the shadows among my cooking pans. Or they would singe their wings and fall, and their hot wings, as if melted, would stick to the first thing they touched—a pan, a lid, a spoon—so that the snagged moths could struggle only in tiny arcs, unable to flutter free. These I could release by a quick flip of a stick; in the morning I would find my cooking stuff decorated with torn flecks of moth wings, ghostly triangles of shiny dust here and there on the aluminum. So I read, and boiled water, and replenished candles, and read on.

One night a moth flew into the candle, was caught, burnt dry, and held. I must have been staring at the candle, or maybe I looked up when a shadow crossed my page; at any rate, I saw it all. A golden female moth, a biggish one with a two-inch wingspread, flapped into the fire, dropped abdomen into the wet wax, stuck, flamed, and frazzled in a second. Her moving wings ignited like tissue paper, like angels' wings, enlarging the circle of light in the clearing and creating out of the darkness the sudden blue sleeves of my sweater, the green leaves of jewelweed by my side, the ragged red trunk of a pine; at once the light contracted again and the moth's wings vanished in a fine, foul smoke. At the same time, her six legs clawed, curled, blackened, and ceased, disappearing utterly. And her head jerked in spasms, making a spattering noise; her antennae crisped and burnt away and her heaving mouthparts cracked like pistol fire. When it was all over, her head was, so far as I could determine, gone, gone the long way of her wings and legs. Her head was hole lost to time. All that was left was the glowing horn shell of her abdomen and thorax—a fraying, partially collapsed gold tube jammed upright in the candle's round pool.

And then this moth-essence, this spectacular skeleton, began to act as a wick. She kept burning. The wax rose in the moth's body from her soaking abdomen to her thorax to the shattered hole where her head should have been, and widened into flame, a saffron-yellow flame that robed her to the ground like an immolating monk. That candle had two wicks, two winding flames of identical light, side by side. The moth's head was fire. She burned for two hours, until I blew her out.

She burned for two hours without changing, without swaying or kneeling—only glowing within, like a building fire glimpsed through silhouetted walls, like a hollow saint, like a flame-faced virgin gone to God, while I read by her light, kindled, while Rimbaud in Paris burnt out his brain in a thousand poems, while night pooled wetly at my feet.

So. That is why I think those hollow shreds on the bathroom floor are moths. I believe I know what moths look like, in any state.

I have three candles here on the table which I disentangle from the plants and light when visitors come. The cats avoid them, although Small's tail caught fire once; I rubbed it out before she noticed. I don't mind living alone. I like eating alone and reading. I don't mind sleeping alone. The only time I mind being alone is when something is funny; then, when I am laughing at something funny, I wish someone were around. Sometimes I think it is pretty funny that I sleep alone.

After reading both essays, how do you think each author feels about the event they witness? What specific words does Woolf use to describe the moth's death? Which words does Dillard employ? How does the narration of the two essays compare to one another?

Using Google or another search engine, search the web for biographical information about Woolf and Dillard. Where were they born? What kind of family and social background did they each come from? Why are they considered such good writers?

In a page or two, compare and contrast Woolf's and Dillard's essays. How are they alike? How are they different? What message do you think each author attempts to convey to the reader? How do you feel after reading these two accounts of the death of a moth?

Physician, poet, and essayist Lewis Thomas had the rare gift of making science interesting and understandable for the average reader. Thomas won numerous awards for his medical research, yet also found time to write poetry good enough to be published in The Atlantic Monthly *and* Harper's Bazaar. *Invited to write essays for the* New England Journal of Medicine, *Thomas went on to publish a number of books bridging the gap between science and literature. The book from which the essay below was taken,* The Medusa and the Snail: More Notes of a Biology Watcher, *won a National Book Award in 1981.*

ON NATURAL DEATH

By Lewis Thomas

There are so many new books about dying that there are now special shelves set aside for them in bookshops, along with the health-diet and home-repair paperbacks and the sex manuals. Some of them are so packed with detailed information and step-by-step instructions for performing the function that you'd think this was a new sort of skill which all of us are now required to learn. The strongest impression the casual reader gets, leafing through, is that proper dying has become extraordinary, even an exotic experience, something only the specially trained get to do.

Also, you could be led to believe that we are the only creatures capable of the awareness of death, that when all the rest of nature is being cycled through dying, one generation after another, it is a different kind of process, done automatically and trivially, more "natural," as we say.

An elm in our backyard caught the blight this summer and dropped stone dead, leafless, almost overnight. One weekend it was a normal-looking elm, maybe a little bare in spots but nothing alarming, and the next weekend it was gone, passed over, departed, taken. Taken is right, for the tree surgeon came by yesterday with his crew of young helpers and their cherry picker, and took it down branch by branch and carted it off in the back of a red truck, everyone singing.

The dying of a field mouse, at the jaws of an amiable household cat, is a spectacle I have beheld many times. It used to make me wince. Early in life

I gave up throwing sticks at the cat to make him drop the mouse, because the dropped mouse regularly went ahead and died anyway, but I always shouted unaffections at the cat to let him know the sort of animal he had become. Nature, I thought, was an abomination.

Recently I've done some thinking about that mouse, and I wonder if his dying is necessarily all that different from the passing of our elm. The main difference, if there is one, would be in the matter of pain. I do not believe that an elm tree has pain receptors, and even so, the blight seems to me a relatively painless way to go even if there were nerve endings in a tree, which there are not. But the mouse dangling tail-down from the teeth of a gray cat is something else again, with pain beyond bearing, you'd think, all over his small body.

There are now some plausible reasons for thinking it is not like that at all, and you can make up an entirely different story about the mouse and his dying if you like. At the instant of being trapped and penetrated by teeth, peptide hormones are released by cells in the hypothalamus and the pituitary gland; instantly these substances, called endorphins, are attached to the surfaces of other cells responsible for pain perception; the hormones have the pharmacologic properties of opium; there is no pain. Thus it is that the mouse seems always to dangle so languidly from the jaws, lies there so quietly when dropped, and dies of his injuries without a struggle. If a mouse could shrug, he'd shrug.

I do not know if this is true or not, nor do I know how to prove it if it is true. Maybe if you could get in there quickly enough and administer naloxone, a specific morphine antagonist, you could turn off the endorphins and observe the restoration of pain, but this is not something I would care to do or see. I think I will leave it there, as a good guess about the dying of a cat-chewed mouse, perhaps about dying in general.

Montaigne had a hunch about dying, based on his own close call in a riding accident. He was so badly injured as to be believed dead by his companions, and was carried home with lamentations, "all bloody, stained all over with the blood I had thrown up." He remembers the entire episode, despite having been "dead, for two full hours," with wonderment:

It seemed to me that my life was hanging only by the tip of my lips. I closed my eyes in order, it seemed me, to help push it out, and took pleasure in growing languid and letting myself go. It was an idea that was only floating on the surface of my soul, as delicate and feeble as all the rest, but in truth not only free from distress but mingled with that sweet feeling that people have who have let themselves slide into sleep. I believe that this is the same state in which people find themselves whom we see fainting in the agony of death, and I maintain that we pity them without cause. . . . In order to get used to the idea of death, I find there is nothing like coming close to it.

Later, in another essay, Montaigne returns to it:

If you know not how to die, never trouble yourself; Nature will in a moment fully and sufficiently instruct you; she will exactly do that business for you; take you no care for it.

The worst accident I've ever seen was on Okinawa, in the early days of the invasion, when a jeep ran into a troop carrier and was crushed nearly flat. Inside were two young MPs, trapped in bent steel, both mortally hurt, with only their heads and shoulders visible. We had a conversation while people with the right tools were prying them free. Sorry about the accident, they said. No, they said, they felt fine. Is everyone else okay, one of them said. Well, the other one said, no hurry now. And then they died.

Pain is useful for avoidance, for getting away when there's time to get away, but when it is end game, and no way back, pain is likely to be turned off, and the mechanisms for this are wonderfully precise and quick. If I had to design an ecosystem in which creatures had to live off each other and in which dying was in indispensable part of living, I could not think of a better way to manage.

Part of our fear of death is our fear of pain, of dying in agony. In this essay, Lewis argues that our bodies have a built-in process to alleviate pain when death is imminent. What is this physical process? According to Lewis, how does it work?

For most people in our society, actual death remains a mystery, given how little we are exposed to it. Here, Lewis quotes the eighteenth century French philosopher and essayist Montaigne, who assures us death is nothing to worry about since "Nature" will, when the time comes, "fully and sufficiently instruct you." In a paragraph or two, give your response to Lewis's account of the natural process of dying. Are you comforted? Why or why not?

excerpt from

R.I.P.: THE COMPLETE BOOK OF DEATH AND DYING

By Constance Jones

THE DYING BRAIN AND THE NEAR-DEATH EXPERIENCE

The lack of oxygen that causes death may also produce the cluster of perceptions known as the near-death experience (NDE). People who appear clinically dead and then are revived report that during the interval of "death," they are aware of events in the immediate vicinity, in the mind or in some realm beyond.

When Raymond Moody first published his collected accounts of such experiences in 1977, most people viewed them as paranormal events that provided evidence of an afterlife. Recent analyses, however, explain NDE neurologically and suggest that the genetic basis for that last conscious moment is, in essence, imprinted in the right temporal lobe and limbic area of the brain. Under the right conditions, if death approaches not too slowly and not too quickly, the patient will experience this moment as a transition rather than as an end. Whether it is indeed a transition or merely the illusion of one is a separate question. Nor is it known how common this experience is, since most potential informants do not return with the data.

The new analyses suggest that the key factor in NDE is the gradual onset of anoxia (oxygen deprivation) in the brain. The effects of anoxia combine with whatever neural activity is going on when the anoxia strikes; both are superimposed on what might be termed a template, found in the right temporal lobe of the brain. The resulting activity may generate or at least correlate to the near-death experience.

Attempting to replicate Moody's findings, psychologist Kenneth Ring collected numerous accounts of NDE and discerned in them a "core experience" of five elements: entering the darkness (the tunnel effect), seeing the light, feelings of peace, body separation (out-of-body experiences) and entering the light. Every NDE did not include all of these elements, but most included at least two.

That such experiences occur is well documented, and many people believe that an NDE offers a glimpse of "the other side" of death. Some scientists, however, have analyzed the experiences to see whether they occur only near death and how else they might be explained.

Melvin Morse, a Seattle physician, began by investigating the near-death experiences of children, a population he believed would be relatively free of preconceptions on the subject. His first study compared 12 children who had cardiac arrests for a variety of reasons with 121 children who had been gravely ill but had no such brush with death. He found that only the first group, those who truly approached death, reported NDEs.

Morse's neurological explanation of NDE derives from the work of the neurologist Wilder Penfield. When operating on the brain, Penfield found that stimulation of an area called the Sylvian fissure, located in the right temporal lobe just above the right ear, produced sensations similar to some aspects of NDE. When he stimulated this area, patients reported out-of-body experiences, seeing dead relatives, seeing God and other elements of the core experience, with the exception of "the light." Morse and his colleagues theorized that NDE is in fact genetically imprinted in that part of the brain. When he published his analysis, he found that a group of Chilean researchers had independently arrived at the same conclusion.

The one aspect of NDE that Morse's theory does not account for is the light that many people report. This light is extraordinary, with a warm, enveloping quality that makes an extremely powerful impression on those who experience it. The light, too, can be explained in neurological terms. Susan Blackmore, a British psychologist, has analyzed NDEs in an effort to discover what physiological mechanisms might explain these apparently mystical experiences. She argues that neither paranormal nor spiritual explanations are necessary to account for the light or any other aspect of NDE. It's all right there in the brain.

Blackmore's explanation, amply supported by her own research and that of others, runs as follows. When brain cells become anoxic, they do not simply stop firing. Rather, what happens is what Blackmore terms "disinhibition," in which many cells that should not be firing start to fire. Under normal circumstances, neurons send chemical signals across the synapses, or gaps between them; these signals either excite the recipient cell or inhibit it. In anoxia, the inhibition function is lost first, hence the random firing. She argues that NDEs are triggered only under some types of anoxia, when onset is neither very fast nor very slow. Under these circumstances, rapid, disorganized firing of nerve cells over large parts of the brain could explain NDE.

The similarities between NDEs reported by different people—the tunnels, the out-of-body experiences, the light and the feelings of well-being—can be explained by the similarity of all human brains. The tunnel effect, Blackmore argues, arises from disinhibition in the visual cortex and relates to the way brain activity translates into images. Cells cluster at the center of the visual field, with fewer at the edges. If cells start firing randomly, more cells will fire at the center simply because there are more of them there. This activity translates into the visual image of a bright circle that appears brighter toward the center. The image will be round because that's how this kind of brain activity "appears." The "end of the tunnel" approaches, according to this theory, because as the "neural noise" produced by the firing cells increases, the light would appear to get bigger. The rushing sound that accompanies the passage down the tunnel likewise is a function of disinhibition.

The feelings of intense well-being reported in many NDEs, Blackmore and others argue, arises when the body releases endorphins, the opiates produced by the brain in response to stress. Investigations by other researchers strongly suggest that endorphins are released near death. Endorphins produce feelings of intense well-being. Interesting, if anecdotal, support for this theory comes from an account of an NDE reported by a 72-year-old man, whose experience of bliss while in a coma suddenly ended when beings of light were transformed into devils. It turned out that he had been given an injection of naloxone to try to rouse him. Naloxone is a potent opiate antagonist, which would have halted the release of the endorphins.

No paranormal explanation is necessary for out-of-body experiences (OBE), although many observers, including some scientists, continue to argue that OBE is a genuine paranormal experience. The literature on NDEs is full of accounts of people whose "spirit," when out of the body, saw and remembered seeing something that the person could not have known happened.

Raymond Moody, however, has concluded that no evidence supports the claim that "something" leaves the body during alleged OBEs. He and other investigators point out that too many non-paranormal explanations remain. These involve the conjunction of memory and information gathered by the five senses even in an apparently unconscious state. Indeed, a visual OBE has never been authoritatively documented in a blind person, whose "astral body" would presumably be sighted.

Endorphins also figure in the neurological explanation of the life review, in which one's whole life flashes before one as death approaches. The life review is not part of the core experience and is reported in only about one-third of NDEs. But since this review is often carried out by "beings of light," it is invoked as evidence that the NDE is indeed paranormal. Again, however, the dying brain theory provides a plausible, if complex, explanation that excludes the paranormal in favor of Wilder Penfield's studies of the temporal lobe. As Blackmore explains it, endorphins are released during stress. One of their effects is to lower the threshold for seizures in the temporal lobe (which Penfield showed to be the source of NDE-like experiences) and the limbic system, the part of the brain that governs feelings and emotions. In epileptics, seizure activity in this area can produce flashbacks and feelings of déjà vu. In NDE, abnormal activity in these areas causes flashbacks and the feelings of familiarity that may make the experience feel so real.

TESTING AND STORING ORGANS FOR TRANSPLANT

As soon after the moment of death as possible, any organs destined for transplantation must be removed. The removal of organs for transplant is like a routine surgical operation, except that the donor is not anesthetized. Known as "harvesting," the removal implies all the abundance and nourishment of a literal harvest, for it offers the recipient life.

Surgeons carry out the procedure in a sterile operating room in which the donor is hooked to life-support machines to keep the heart beating. Because of the life-support system, the organs are still receiving oxygen through the blood. The sequence of the operation depends on the number of organs the decedent is donating. If only one organ is being removed, the surgeons remove it and close the incision. When multiple organs are being removed, successive teams of surgeons move in and harvest the organs separately.

At times, the recipient of the organ waits, prepped for surgery, in a nearby operating room. More often, however, the organ must be packed up and transported as quickly as possible to the recipient's hospital. The need for speedy transport means that most donated organs go to people who live nearby. How long an organ remains viable for transplant depends on the organ. A heart-lung combination must reach the recipient in four to five hours, while in kidney transplants the interval may extend as long as 48 to 72 hours. A heart alone may be transplanted six to eight hours later and lungs along up to 12 hours later.

Tissue donation is an equally important but less urgent process. A tissue may be removed after the physicians turn off the life-support system and kept for much longer before being transplanted. These include corneas, bones, skin, veins and heart valves.

TISSUE DISPOSAL AND CONTAGION

Any tissue that will not be transplanted from a corpse into a living recipient must be disposed of in some manner. Such disposal, and the manner in which it is carried out, for the most part serves more of a cultural than a public health function. Although many cultures and religions view dead bodies as unclean, today's dead pose no threat to the health of the living except in highly unusual circumstances.

According to Jones, what is a near-death experience? What are the most common elements of a NDE? What scientific explanations does Jones provide to account for near-death experiences?

Using Google or another search engine, search the web for sites that discuss near-death experiences. What other explanations can you find to account for a NDE? For those who believe near-death experiences are supernatural, or paranormal, what reasons do they put forward to explain why these occur?

Working together in groups, using the resources of your campus library and/or the Internet, list any books and films you find that depict a NDE. How many of these provide a scientific explanation? A paranormal one?

Author and freelance writer Mary Roach began her writing career with a public relations job for the San Francisco Zoological Society. Her articles have appeared in National Geographic *and the* New York Times *magazine. Her book,* Stiff, *grew out of an article she did for Salon.com. Stiff, excerpted below, was selected for the Washington State Common Reading program for 2008–2009.*

excerpt from

STIFF: THE CURIOUS LIVES OF HUMAN CADAVERS

By Mary Roach

LIFE AFTER DEATH

On human decay and what can be done about it

Out behind the University of Tennessee Medical Center is a lovely, forested grove with squirrels leaping in the branches of hickory trees and birds calling and patches of green grass where people lie on their backs in the sun, or sometimes the shade, depending on where the researchers put them.

This pleasant Knoxville hillside is a field research facility, the only one in the world dedicated to the study of human decay. The people lying in the sun are dead. They are donated cadavers, helping, in their mute, fragrant way, to advance the science of criminal forensics. For the more you know about how dead bodies decay—the biological and chemical phases they go through, how long each phase lasts, how the environment affects these phases—the better equipped you are to figure out when any given body died: in other words, the day and even the approximate time of day it was murdered. The police are pretty good at pinpointing approximate time of death in recently dispatched bodies. The potassium level of the gel inside the eyes is helpful during the first twenty-four hours, as is algor mortis—the cooling of a dead body; barring temperature extremes, corpses lose about 1.5 degrees Fahrenheit per hour until they reach the temperature of the air around them. (Rigor mortis is more variable: It starts a few hours after death, usually in the head and neck, and continues, moving on down the body, finishing up and disappearing anywhere from ten to forty-eight hours after death.)

If a body has been dead longer than three days, investigators turn to entomological clues (e.g., how old are these fly larvae?) and stages of decay for their answers. And decay is highly dependent on environmental and situational factors. What's the weather been like? Was the body buried? In what? Seeking better understanding of the effects of these factors, the University of Tennessee (UT) Anthropological Research Facility, as it is blandly and vaguely called, has buried bodies in shallow graves, encased them in concrete, left them in car trunks and man-made ponds, and wrapped them in plastic bags. Pretty much anything a killer might do to dispose of a dead body the researchers at UT have done also.

To understand how these variables affect the time line of decomposition, you must be intimately acquainted with your control scenario: basic, unadulterated human decay. That's why I'm here. That's what I want to know: When you let nature take its course, just exactly what course does it take?

My guide to the world of human disassembly is a patient, amiable man named Arpad Vass. Vass has studied the science of human decomposition for more than a decade. He is an adjunct research professor of forensic anthropology at UT and a senior staff scientist at the nearby Oak Ridge National Laboratory. One of Arpad's projects at ORNL has been to develop a method of pinpointing time of death by analyzing tissue samples from the victim's organs and measuring the amounts of dozens of different time-dependent decay chemicals. This profile of decay chemicals is then matched against the typical profiles for that tissue for each passing postmortem hour. In test runs, Arpad's method has determined the time of death to within plus or minus twelve hours.

The samples he used to establish the various chemical breakdown time lines came from bodies at the decay facility. Eighteen bodies, some seven hundred samples in all. It was an unspeakable task, particularly in the later stages of decomposition, and particularly for certain organs. "We'd have to roll the bodies over to get at the liver," recalls Arpad. The brain he got to using a probe through the eye orbit. Interestingly, neither of these activities was responsible for Arpad's closest brush with on-the-job regurgitation. "One day last summer," he says weakly, "I *inhaled* a fly. I could feel it buzzing down my throat."

I have asked Arpad what it's like to do this sort of work. "What do you mean?" he asked me back. "You want a vivid description of what's going through my brain as I'm cutting through a liver and all these larvae are spilling out all over me and juice pops out of the intestines?" I kind of did, but I kept quiet. He went on: "I don't really focus on that. I try to focus on the value of the work. It takes the edge off the grotesqueness." As for the humanness of his specimens, that no longer disturbs him. Though it once did. He used to lay the bodies on their stomachs so he didn't have to see their faces.

This morning, Arpad and I are riding in the back of a van being driven by the lovable and agreeable Ron Walli, one of ORNL's media relations guys. Ron pulls into a row of parking spaces at the far end of the UT Medical Center lot, labeled G section. On hot summer days, you can always find a parking space in G section, and not just because it's a longer walk to the hospital. G section is bordered by a tall wooden fence topped with concertina wire, and on the other side of the fence are the bodies. Arpad steps down from the van. "Smell's not that bad today," he says. His "not that bad" has that hollow, over-upbeat tone one hears when spouses back over flowerbeds or home hair coloring goes awry.

Ron, who began the trip in a chipper mood, happily pointing out landmarks and singing along with the radio, has the look of a condemned man. Arpad sticks his head in the window. "Are you coming in, Ron, or are you going to hide in the car again?" Ron steps out and glumly follows. Although this is his fourth time in, he says he'll never get used to it. It's not the fact that they're dead—Ron saw accident victims routinely in his former post as a newspaper reporter—it's the sights and smells of decay. "The smell just stays with you," he says. "Or that's what you imagine. I must have washed my hands and face twenty times after I got back from my first time out here."

Just inside the gate are two old-fashioned metal mailboxes on posts, as though some of the residents had managed to convince the postal service that death, like rain or sleet or hail, should not stay the regular delivery of the U.S. Mail. Arpad opens one and pulls turquoise rubber surgical gloves from a box, two for him and two for me. He knows not to offer them to Ron.

"Let's start over there." Arpad is pointing to a large male figure about twenty feet distant. From this distance, he could be napping, though there is something in the lay of the arms and the stillness of him that suggests something more permanent. We walk toward the man. Ron stays near the gate, feigning interest in the construction details of a toolshed.

Like many big-bellied people in Tennessee, the dead man is dressed for comfort. He wears gray sweatpants and a single-pocket white T-shirt. Arpad explains that one of the graduate students is studying the effects of clothing on the decay process. Normally, they are naked.

The cadaver in the sweatpants is the newest arrival. He will be our poster man for the first stage of human decay, the "fresh" stage. ("Fresh," as in fresh fish, not fresh air. As in recently dead but not necessarily something you want to put your nose right up to.) The hallmark of fresh-stage decay is a process called autolysis, or self-digestion. Human cells use enzymes to cleave molecules, breaking compounds down into things they can use. While a person is alive, the cells keep these enzymes in check, preventing them from breaking down the cells' own walls. After death, the enzymes operate unchecked and begin eating through the cell structure, allowing the liquid inside to leak out.

"See the skin on his fingertips there?" says Arpad. Two of the dead man's fingers are sheathed with what look like rubber fingertips of the sort worn by accountants and clerk. "The liquid from the cells gets between the layers of skin and loosens them. As that progresses, you see skin sloughage." Mortuary types have a different name for this. They call it "skin slip." Sometimes the skin of the entire hand will come off. Mortuary types don't have a name for this, but forensics types do. It's called "gloving."

"As the process progresses, you see giant sheets of skin peeling off the body," says Arpad. He pulls up the hem of the man's shirt to see if, indeed, giant sheets are peeling. They are not, and that's okay.

Something else is going on. Squirming grains of rice are crowded into the man's belly button. It's a rice grain mosh pit. But rice grains do not move. These cannot be grains of rice. They are not. They are young flies. Entomologists have a name for young flies, but it is an ugly name, an insult. Let's not use the word "maggot." Let's use a pretty word. Let's use "hacienda."

Arpad explains that the flies lay their eggs on the body's points of entry: the eyes, the mouth, open wounds, genitalia. Unlike older, larger haciendas, the little ones can't eat through skin. I make the mistake of asking Arpad what the little haciendas are after.

Arpad walks around to the corpse's left foot. It is bluish and the skin is transparent. "See the [haciendas] under the skin? They're eating the subcutaneous fat. They love fat." I see them. They are spaced out, moving slowly. It's kind of beautiful, this man's skin with these tiny white slivers embedded just beneath its surface. It looks like expensive Japanese rice paper. You tell yourself these things.

Let us return to the decay scenario. The liquid that is leaking from the enzyme-ravaged cells is now making its way through the body. Soon enough it makes contact with the body's bacteria colonies: the ground troops of putrefaction. These bacteria were there in the living body as well, in the intestinal tract, in the lungs, on the skin—the places that came in contact with the outside world. Life is looking rosy for our one-celled friends. They've already been enjoying the benefits of a decommissioned human immune system, and now, suddenly, they're awash with this edible goo, issuing from the ruptured cells of the intestinal lining. It's raining food. As will happen in times of plenty, the population swells. Some of the bacteria migrate to the far frontiers of the body, traveling by sea, afloat in the same liquid that keeps them nourished. Soon bacteria are everywhere. The scene is set for stage two: bloat.

The life of a bacterium is built around food. Bacteria don't have mouths or fingers or Wolf Ranges, but they eat. They digest. They excrete. Like us, they break their food down into its more elemental components. The enzymes in our stomachs break meat down into proteins. The bacteria in our gut break those proteins down into amino acids; they take up where we leave off. When we die, they stop feeding on what we've eaten and begin feeding on us. And, just as they do when we're alive, they produce gas in the process. Intestinal gas is a waste product of bacteria metabolism.

The difference is that when we're alive, we expel that gas. The dead, lacking workable stomach muscles and sphincters and bedmates to annoy, do not. Cannot. So the gas builds up and the belly bloats. I ask Arpad why the gas wouldn't just get forced out eventually. He explains that the small intestine has pretty much collapsed and sealed itself off. Or that there might be "something" blocking its egress. Though he allows, with some prodding, that a little bad air often does, in fact, slip out, and so, as a matter of record, it can be said that dead people fart. It needn't be, but it can.

Arpad motions me to follow him up the path. He knows where a good example of the bloat stage can be found.

Ron is still down by the shed, affecting some sort of gratuitous lawn mower maintenance, determined to avoid the sights and smells beyond the gate. I call for him to join me. I feel the need for company, someone else who doesn't see this sort of thing every day. Ron follows, looking at his sneakers. We pass a skeleton six feet seven inches tall and dressed in a red Harvard sweatshirt and sweatpants. Ron's eyes stay on his shoes. We pass a woman whose sizable breasts have decomposed, leaving only the skins, like flattened bota bags upon her chest. Ron's eyes stay on his shoes.

Bloat is most noticeable in the abdomen, Arpad is saying, where the largest numbers of bacteria are, but it happens in other bacterial hot spots, most notably the mouth and genitalia. "In the male, the penis and especially the testicles can become very large."

"Like how large?" (Forgive me.)

"I don't know. Large."

"Softball large? Watermelon large?"

"Okay, softball." Arpad Vass is a man with infinite reserves of patience, but we are scraping the bottom of the tank.

Arpad continues. Bacteria-generated gas bloats the lips and the tongue, the latter often to the point of making it protrude from the mouth: In real life as it is in cartoons. The eyes do not bloat because the liquid long ago leached out. They are gone. Xs. In real life as it is in cartoons.

Arpad stops and looks down. "That's bloat." Before us is a man with a torso greatly distended. It is of a circumference I more readily associate with livestock. As for the groin, it is difficult to tell what's going on; insects cover the area, like something he is wearing. The face is similarly obscured. The larvae are two weeks older than their peers down the hill and much larger. Where before they had been grains of rice, here they are cooked rice. They live like rice, too, pressed together: a moist, solid entity. If you lower your head to within a foot or two of an infested corpse (and this I truly don't recommend), you can hear them feeding. Arpad pinpoints the sound: "Rice Krispies." Ron frowns. Ron used to like Rice Krispies.

Bloat continues until something gives way. Usually it is the intestines. Every now and then, it is the torso itself. Arpad has never seen it, but he has heard it, twice. "A rending, ripping noise" is how he describes it. Bloat is typically short-lived, perhaps a week and it's over. The final stage, putrefaction and decay, lasts longest.

Putrefaction refers to the breaking down and gradual liquefaction of tissue by bacteria. It is going on during the bloat phase—for the gas that bloats a body is being created by the breakdown of tissue—but its effects are not yet obvious.

Arpad continues up the wooded slope. "This woman over here is farther along," he says. That's a nice way to say it. Dead people, unembalmed ones anyway, basically dissolve; they collapse and sink in upon themselves and eventually seep out onto the ground. Do you recall the Margaret Hamilton death scene in *The Wizard of Oz*? ("I'm melting!") Putrefaction is more or less a slowed-down version of this. The woman lies in a mud of her own making. Her torso appears sunken, its organs gone—leached out onto the ground around her.

The digestive organs and the lungs disintegrate first, for they are home to the greatest numbers of bacteria; the larger your work crew, the faster the building comes down. The brain is another early-departure organ. "Because all the bacteria in the mouth chew through the palate," explains Arpad. And because brains are soft and easy to eat. "The brain liquefies very quickly. It just pours out the ears and bubbles out the mouth."

Up until about three weeks, Arpad says, remnants of organs can still be identified. "After that, it becomes like a soup in there." Because he knew I was going to ask, Arpad adds, "Chicken soup. It's yellow."

Ron turns on his heels. "Great." We ruined Rice Krispies for Ron, and now we have ruined chicken soup.

Muscles are eaten not only by bacteria, but by carnivorous beetles. I wasn't aware that meat-eating beetles existed, but there you go. Sometimes the skin gets eaten, sometimes not. Sometimes, depending on the weather, it dries out and mummifies, whereupon it is too tough for just about anyone's taste. On our way out, Arpad shows us a skeleton with mummified skin, lying facedown. The skin has remained on the legs as far as the tops of the ankles. The torso, likewise, is covered, about up to the shoulder blades. The edge of the skin is curved, giving the appearance of a scooped neckline, as on a dancer's leotard. Though naked, he seems dressed. The outfit is not as colorful or, perhaps, warm as a Harvard sweatsuit, but more fitting for the venue.

We stand for a minute, looking at the man.

There is a passage in the Buddhist Sutra on Mindfulness called the Nine Cemetery Contemplations. Apprentice monks are instructed to mediate on a series of decomposing bodies in the charnel ground, starting with a body "swollen and blue and festering," progressing to one "being eaten by . . . different kinds of worms," and moving on to a skeleton, "without flesh and blood, held together by the tendons." The monks were told to keep meditating until they were calm and a smile appeared on their faces. I describe this to Arpad and Ron, explaining that the idea is to come to peace with the transient nature of our bodily existence, to overcome the revulsion and fear. Or something.

We all stare at the man. Arpad swats at flies.

"So," says Ron. "Lunch?"

Outside the gate, we spend a long time scraping the bottoms of our boots on a curb. You don't have to step on a body to carry the smells of death with you on your shoes. For reasons we have just seen, the soil around a corpse is sodden with the liquids of human decay. By analyzing the chemicals in this soil, people like Arpad can tell if a body has been moved from where it decayed. If the unique volatile fatty acids and compounds of human decay aren't there, the body didn't decompose there.

One of Arpad's graduate students, Jennifer Love, has been working on an aroma scan technology for estimating time of death. Based on a technology used in the food and wine industries, the device, now being funded by the FBI, would be a sort of hand-held electronic nose that could be waved over a body and used to identify the unique odor signature that a corpse put off at different stages of decay.

I tell them that the Ford Motor Company developed an electronic nose programmed to identify acceptable "new car smell." Car buyers expect their purchases to smell a certain way: leathery and new, but with no vinyl off-gassy smells. The nose makes sure the cars comply. Arpad observes that the new-car smell electronic nose probably uses a technology similar to what the electronic nose for cadavers would use.

"Just don't get 'em confused," deadpans Ron. He is imagining a young couple, back from a test drive, the woman turning to her husband and saying: "You know, that car smelled like a dead person."

It is difficult to put words to the smell of decomposing human. It is dense and cloying, sweet but not flower-sweet. Halfway between rotting fruit and rotting meat. On my walk home each afternoon, I pass a fetid little produce store that gets the mix almost right, so much so that I find myself peering behind the papaya bins for an arm or a glimpse of naked feet. Barring a visit to my neighborhood, I would direct the curious to a chemical supply company, from which one can order synthetic versions of many of these volatiles. Arpad's lab has rows of labeled glass vials: Skatole, Indole, Putrescine, Cadaverine. The moment wherein I uncorked the putrescine in his office may well be the moment he began looking forward to my departure. Even if you've never been around a decaying body, you've smelled putrescine. Decaying fish throws off putrescine, a fact I learned from a gripping *Journal of Food Science* article entitled "Post-Mortem Changes in Black Skipjack Muscle During Storage in Ice." This fits in with something Arpad told me. He said he knew a company that manufactured a putrescine detector, which doctors could use in place of swabs and cultures to diagnose vaginitis or, I suppose, a job at the skipjack cannery.

The market for synthetic putrescine and cadaverine is small, but devoted. The handlers of "human remains dogs" use these compounds for training[1] Human remains dogs are distinct from the dogs that search for escaped felons and the dogs that search for whole cadavers. They are trained to alert their owners

---

[1] Purists among them insist on the real deal. I spent an afternoon in an abandoned dormitory at Moffett Air Force Base, watching one such woman, Shirley Hammond, put her canine noses through their paces. Hammond is a fixture on the base, regularly seen walking to and from her car with a pink gym bag and a plastic cooler. If you were to ask her what she's got in there, and she chose to answer you honestly, the answer would go more or less like this: a bloody shirt, dirt from beneath a decomposed corpse, human tissue buried in a chunk of cement, a piece of cloth rubbed on cadavers, a human molar. No synthetics for Shirley's dogs.

when they detect the specific scents of decomposed human tissue. They can pinpoint the location of a corpse at the bottom of a lake by sniffing the water's surface for the gases and fats that float up from the rotting remains. They can detect the lingering scent molecules of a decomposing body up to fourteen months after the killer lugged it away.

I had trouble believing this when I heard it. I no longer have trouble. The soles of my boots, despite washing and soaking in Clorox, would smell of corpse for months after my visit.

Ron drives us and our little cloud of stink to a riverside restaurant for lunch. The hostess is young and pink and clean-looking. Her plump forearms and tight-fitting skin are miracles. I imagine her smelling of talcum powder and shampoo, the light, happy smells of the living. We stand apart from the hostess and the other customers, as though we were traveling with an ill-tempered, unpredictable dog. Arpad signals to the hostess that we are three. Four, if you count The Smell.

"Would you like to sit indoors . . . ?"

Arpad cuts her off. "Outdoors. And away from people."

That is the story of human decay. I would wager that if the good people of the eighteenth and nineteenth centuries had known what happens to dead bodies in the sort of detail that you and I now know, dissection might not have seemed so uniquely horrific. Once you've seen bodies dissected, and once you've seen them decomposing, the former doesn't seem so dreadful. Yes, the people of the eighteenth and nineteenth centuries were buried, but that only served to draw out the process. Even in a coffin six feet deep, the body eventually decomposes. Not all the bacteria living in a human body require oxygen; there are plenty of anaerobic bacteria up to the task.

In our culture, there is no more veiled aspect of death than the decay of the human body. After all, no one wants to contemplate, much less witness, the physical decay of the body of a friend or family member. And since the laws in most states require dead bodies be embalmed, we have little first-hand experience of the natural process of decay. According to Roach, what are the stages a human body goes through as it decomposes? Why study such a gruesome topic?

Television shows like *CSI* and *Bones* have made the forensic study of dead bodies popular. Using Google or another search engine, search the web for sites that define and discuss the field of forensic science. What does a forensic scientist do? What are the educational requirements? What universities offer degrees in forensic science? What areas of specialization are available for someone in forensic science?

Death

English-born author and investigative journalist Jessica Mitford was born the daughter of an English aristocrat, Baron Redesdale. Rebelling against her family's support of Hitler, in 1944 she became an American citizen. An activist in the civil rights movement, Mitford was a harsh critic of both the American prison system and the funeral industry. Her 1963 book, The American Way of Death, prompted congressional hearings into the funeral industry. She died in 1998 and her funeral is reported to have cost a mere $533.31.

excerpt from

THE AMERICAN WAY OF DEATH, REVISITED

BY JESSICA MITFORD

How long, I would ask, are we to be subjected to the tyranny of custom and undertakers? Truly, it is all vanity and vexation of spirit—a mere mockery of woe, costly to all, far, far beyond its value; and ruinous to many; hateful, and an abomination to all; yet submitted to by all, because none have the moral courage to speak against it and act in defiance of it.

—Lord Essex

O death, where is thy sting? O grave, where is thy victory? Where, indeed. Many a badly stung survivor, faced with the aftermath of some relative's funeral, has ruefully concluded that the victory has been won hands down by a funeral establishment—in a disastrously unequal battle.

Much fun has been poked at some of the irrational "status symbols" set out like golden snares to trap the unwary consumer at every turn. Until recently, little has been said about the most irrational and weirdest of the lot, lying in ambush for all of us at the end of the road—the modern American funeral.

If the Dismal Traders (as an eighteenth-century English writer calls them) have traditionally been cast in a comic role in literature, a universally recognized symbol of humor from Shakespeare to Dickens to Evelyn Waugh, they have successfully turned the tables in recent years to perpetrate a huge, macabre, and expensive practical joke on the American public. It is not consciously conceived of as a joke, of course; on the contrary, it is hedged with admirably contrived rationalizations.

Gradually, almost imperceptibly, over the years the funeral men have constructed their own grotesque cloud-cuckoo-land where the trappings of Gracious Living are transformed, as in a nightmare, into the trappings of Gracious Dying. The same familiar Madison Avenue language, with its peculiar adjectival range designed to anesthetize sales resistance to all sorts of products, has seeped into the funeral industry in a new and bizarre guise. The emphasis is on the same desirable qualities that we have been schooled to look for in our daily search for excellence: comfort, durability, beauty, craftsmanship. The attuned ear will recognize, too, the convincing quasi-scientific language, so reassuring even if unintelligible.

So that this too too solid flesh might not melt, we are offered "solid copper—a quality casket which offers superb value to the client seeking long-lasting protection," or "the Colonial Classic beauty—18 gauge lead coated steel, seamless top, lap-jointed welded body construction." Some are equipped with foam rubber, some with innerspring mattresses. Batesville offers "beds that lift and tilt." Not every casket need have a silver lining, for one may choose among a rich assortment of "color-matched shades" in nonabrasive fabrics. Shrouds no longer exist. Instead, you may patronize a grave-wear couturiere who promises "handmade original fashions—styles from the best in life for the last memory-dresses, men's suits, negligees, accessories." For the final, perfect grooming: "Nature-Glo—the ultimate in cosmetic embalming." And where have we heard that phrase "peace-of-mind protection" before? No matter. In funeral advertising, it is applied to the Wilbert Burial Vault, with its 3/8-inch precast asphalt inner liner plus extra-thick, reinforced concrete—all this "guaranteed by Good Housekeeping." Here again the Cadillac, status symbol par excellence, appears in all its gleaming glory, this time transformed into a sleek funeral hearse. Although lesser vehicles are now used to collect the body and the permits, the Cad is still the conveyance of choice for the Loved One's last excursion to the grave.

You, the potential customer for all this luxury, are unlikely to read the lyrical descriptions quoted above, for they are culled from *Mortuary Management* and other trade magazines of the industry. For you there are the ads in your daily newspaper, generally found on the obituary page, stressing dignity, refinement, high-caliber professional service, and that intangible quality, sincerity. The trade advertisements are, however, instructive, because they furnish an important clue to the frame of mind into which the funeral industry has hypnotized itself.

A new mythology, essential to the twentieth-century American funeral rite, has grown up—or rather has been built up step-by-step—to justify the peculiar customs surrounding the disposal of our dead. And just as the witch doctor must be convinced of his own infallibility in order to maintain a hold over his clientele, so the funeral industry has had to "sell itself" on its articles of faith in the course of passing them along to the public.

The first of these is the tenet that today's funeral procedures are founded in "American tradition." The story comes to mind of a sign on the freshly sown lawn of a brand-new Midwestern college: "There is a tradition on this campus that students never walk on this strip of grass. This tradition goes into effect next Tuesday." The most cursory look at American funerals of past times will establish the parallel. Simplicity to the point of starkness, the plain pine box, the laying out of the dead by friends and family who also bore the coffin to the grave—these were the hallmarks of the traditional American funeral until the end of the nineteenth century.

Secondly, there is the myth that the American public is only being given what it wants—an opportunity to keep up with the Joneses to the end. "In keeping with our high standard of living, there should be an equally high standard of dying," says an industry leader. "The cost of a funeral varies according to individual taste and the niceties of living the family has been accustomed to." Actually, choice doesn't enter the picture for average individuals faced, generally for the first time, with the necessity of buying a product of which they are totally ignorant, at a moment when they are least in a position to quibble. In point of fact, the cost of a funeral almost always varies, not "according to individual taste" but according to what the traffic will bear.

Thirdly, there is an assortment of myths based on half-digested psychiatric theories. The importance of the "memory picture" is stressed—meaning the last glimpse of the deceased in an open casket, done up with the latest in embalming techniques and finished off with a dusting of makeup. Another, impressively authentic-sounding, is the need for "grief therapy," which is big now in mortuary circles. A historian of American funeral directing hints at the grief-therapist idea when speaking of the new role of the undertaker—"the dramaturgic role, in which the undertaker becomes a stage manager to create an appropriate atmosphere and to move the funeral party through a drama in which social relationships are stressed and an emotional catharsis or release is provided through ceremony."

Lastly, a whole new terminology, as ornately shoddy as the rayon satin casket liner, has been invented by the funeral industry to replace the direct and serviceable vocabulary of former times. "Undertaker" has been supplanted by "funeral director" or "mortician." (Even the classified section of the telephone directory gives recognition to this; in its pages you will find "Undertakers—see Funeral Directors.") Coffins are "caskets"; hearses are "coaches" or "professional cars"; flowers are "floral tributes"; corpses generally are "loved ones," but mortuary etiquette dictates that a specific corpse be referred to by name only—as "Mr. Jones"; cremated ashes are "cremains." Euphemisms such as "slumber room," reposing room," and "calcination—the kindlier heat" abound in the funeral business.

If the undertaker is the stage manager of the fabulous production that is the modern American funeral, the stellar role is reserved for the occupant of the open casket. The decor, the stagehands, the supporting cast are all arranged for the most advantageous display of the deceased, without which the rest of the paraphernalia would lose its point—Hamlet without the Prince of Denmark. It is to this end that a fantastic array of costly merchandise and services is pyramided to dazzle the mourners and facilitate the plunder of the next of kin.

Grief therapy, anyone? But it's going to come high. According to the funeral industry's own figures, the average undertaker's bill—$750 in 1961 for casket and "services"—is now $4,700, to which must be added the cost of a burial vault, flowers, clothing, clergy and musician's honorarium, and cemetery charges. When these costs are added to the undertaker's bill, the total cost for an adult's funeral today is $7,800.

The question naturally arises, is this what most people want for themselves and their families? For several reasons, this has been a hard one to answer until recently. It is a subject seldom discussed. Those who have never had to arrange for a funeral frequently shy away from its implications, preferring to take comfort in the thought that sufficient unto the day is the evil thereof.

Those who have acquired personal and painful knowledge of the subject would often rather forget about it. Pioneering "funeral societies" or "memorial associations" dedicated to the principle of funerals at reasonable cost do exist in a number of communities throughout the country, but until recently their membership was limited to the more sophisticated element in the population—university people, liberal intellectuals—and those who, like doctors and lawyers, come up against problems in arranging funerals for their clients.

Some indication of the pent-up resentment felt by vast numbers of people against the funeral interests was furnished by the astonishing response to Roul Tunley's 1961 *Saturday Evening Post* article. As though a dike had burst, letters poured in from every part of the country to the funeral societies, to local newspapers. They came from clergymen, professional people, old-age pensioners, trade unionists. Three months after the article appeared, an estimated six thousand had taken pen in hand to comment on some phase of the high cost of dying. Many recounted their own bitter experiences at the hands of funeral directors; hundreds asked for advice on how to establish a consumer organization in communities where none exists; others sought information about prepayment plans. Thirty years later, the situation seems worse. In 1993 I wrote a letter encouraging funeral simplicity which appeared in a "Dear Abby" column. More than thirty thousand people wrote asking for information about funeral-planning societies. The funeral industry, finding itself in the glare of the public spotlight, continues to engage in serious debate about its own future course—as well it might.

Some entrepreneurs are already testing the waters with stripped-down, low-cost operations. One, calling itself "Church and Chapel Funeral Service," contracts with conventional funeral homes to lower costs by doing the unthinkable—moving the service out of the mortuary to a church, a cemetery chapel, even a nursing home.

In 1994 Russ Harman launched Affordable Funeral Service in a Washington, D.C., suburb. Taking the low-cost approach to the extreme, he operates with no facilities outside his own home. He uses private residences, churches, or, if viewing the deceased is desired, a rented mortuary. The basic strategy, according to Ron Hast's *Funeral Monitor*, is to keep overhead low. A white, unmarked van is used instead of a hearse. There are no limos. Business is booming, with three vans patrolling the nation's capital and lone vans in five other cities. Harman's next project is to take the operation nationwide. Will

Affordable Funeral Service be able to do it? Is seems likely, since late word is that it has been swooped into the net of SCI.

Is the funeral inflation bubble ripe for bursting? Back in the sixties, the American public suddenly rebelled against the trend in the auto industry towards ever more showy cars, with their ostentatious and nonfunctional fins, and a demand was created for compact cars patterned after European models. The all-powerful U.S. auto industry, accustomed to telling customers what sort of car they wanted, was suddenly forced to listen for a change. Overnight, the little cars became for millions a new kind of status symbol. Could it be that the same cycle is working itself out in the attitude towards the final return of dust to dust, that the American public is becoming sickened by ever more ornate and costly funerals, and that a status symbol of the future may indeed be the simplest kind of "funeral without fins"?

According to Mitford, before the end of the nineteenth century, American funerals were simple and inexpensive. What is the average cost of a funeral today? How have funerals changed? Explain.

Using Google or another search engine, search the web for the cost of buying a casket online, starting with http://www.walmart.com. How much of a mark-up do some of these sites claim is added when buying a casket from a funeral home?

Working together in groups, using the resources of your campus library and/or the Internet, research the ways other cultures, both past and present, have honored their dead. What happens to the bodies? How do friends and families respond? What kinds of rituals are practiced? Is there a belief in an afterlife? Explain.

Mitford's article exposes some of the more outrageous and costly practices done for funerals, such as caskets with "inner-spring mattresses" and "handmade original fashions" to dress the dead body. What do you think is important for a funeral? Write a short essay—3 to 5 paragraphs—outlining how you would like your own funeral to be planned, especially in terms of cost.

Former video journalist and radio producer for the Canadian Broadcasting Corporation, Tom Jokinen quit at age forty-four to become an apprentice undertaker at a family-run funeral home in Winnipeg, Manitoba. The excerpt below is from the book Curtains: Adventures of an Undertaker-in-Training that resulted from his experience learning to care for the dead.

excerpt from

CURTAINS: ADVENTURES OF AN UNDERTAKER-IN-TRAINING

BY TOM JOKINEN

LOVE YOUR HAIR, WHO'S YOUR EMBALMER?

To get to the Silver Doors at St. Boniface General Hospital I rattle the stretcher down a long corridor, always empty of people but full of discarded hospital gear: iron bed frames, armless armchairs, IV racks. At St. B the Silver Doors can handle a dozen or more plastic-wrapped corpses comfortably. The security guard has waxy yellow smoker's hair and a lot of questions about working in a crematorium.

"The teeth," he says. "What do you do with them?"

"What do you mean?" I say, checking name tags.

"The *teeth*," he says, and then taps his own in case I'm fuzzy on the concept. "Gold teeth, You pull them out, no?"

"Why would we do that?"

"For the gold."

My corpse is tall, his feet hanging past the end of the gurney. I rip a hole in the plastic sheet and check for jewelry.

"We don't pull out any teeth," I say, but the guard smiles and winks, picturing me, I can tell, with a pair of pliers and my foot on someone's jaw. This is how people see us, if in fact I'm an "us" yet. Gothic weirdos and alchemists, the so-called Dismal Traders, with a bucket full of teeth we put under our pillows to hose the Tooth Fairy.

"I guess I'll have to take out my own," he says.

"That's probably a good idea."

At the Factory, pulling out the stretcher with the tall man strapped into it, I trigger the collapsing legs just as I was taught, forgetting that I was taught to trigger the collapsing legs on the way into the van, not on the way out. Collapsing the legs on the way out is bad. I know this from experience. The stretcher drops, head first, again, hitting the floor, leaving me to stand with the foot-end in my hands while Jon rushes out to see what all the noise is about. This turns out to be a company record: two dropped bodies by a single funeral assistant in a supporting role. Maybe I'll get a plaque on the wall of the lunchroom.

Nat tells me to change into scrubs and meet her in the prep room, and to put some Blistex under my nose if I have any, to kill the smell, until I get used to it—although, she says, you never get used to it. This is my penance for dropping the tall man. Now I have to help embalm him.

I don't have my own scrubs so she issues me a purple set that belonged to an embalmer who used to work here but left after an incident involving his wristwatch. Nat says she accidentally knocked the watch off a shelf in the dressing room. In response he tore off his clothes and ran through the parking lot in his boxers, took her to small-claims court for the cost of repairs, and quit his job. I think he had bigger problems than the watch, she says.

The prep room is smaller than in my workplace nightmares. The walls are white tile, and most of the space is taken up by a steel table, underneath which is a toilet, a lidless American Standard toilet. I know a toilet when I see one. I just didn't expect to see one here. The shelves are stacked with colorful liquids, oranges and reds and purples and milky pinks, just like the bottle in the *Canadian Funeral News* ad. Below the shelves, next to a sink, are the tools, tweezers bent and straight, probes and hooks and pokers and scissors, a cardful of bobby pins, Gillette disposable razors and a pump bottle of Helene Curtis ThermaSilk shampoo. Charts on the wall show the circulatory system in red and blue rivers, mapping a human-shaped continent. Nat and I slide the body from the stretcher onto the table and she sprays it down with blue Dis-Spray, which smells of rubbing alcohol. Both of us are dressed head to feet in splatter gear: scrubs, a paper bonnet, a plastic face-guard, a surgical mask to keep from inhaling chemical fumes.

You never know what you're going to get when you open the shroud, she says. Could be a bloody accident victim, or an old lady with no teeth, her mouth wide open. Nat's enjoying this. She loves the prep room and she wants others to love it too. With a snap she reveals a handsome bald gentleman, half smiling. His eyes are open, one more than the other, but they're dry and foggy. This is the unembalmed, undecorated, raw look of death. I take a close look. If he could be said to have an expression, it would be one of dopey curiosity, upper lip curled, as if he were trying to remember where he left his car keys. Maybe this is how it happens. You make a sandwich, you scratch your ear with a butter knife, you try to remember where the keys are and then *whack*: lights out, forever. In any case, our job is to massage and prod and infuse the man back to a more palatable appearance. We start with a thorough washing.

Nat hoses him down, then soaps his head and encourages me to clean his fingernails with a file and a J-Cloth. The radio on the wall plays the Foo Fighters and she sings along.

"That's just the way life is . . ." goes the chorus.

His skin is yellow and cold. To prepare him for infusion we have to "break rigor," which means bending his arms and legs at the joints to rid them of their natural post-mortem stiffness. Natalie cranks his arm over his head as if it were a rusty pump handle. I lift a leg, foot to ceiling, yoga-style. It's hard, heavy, physical work. The joints are seized, even his fingers, which we massage until they're no longer clenched. The man maintains the dim smile as if he's enjoying this, and issues a dribble of brown drool the color of weak coffee, which Nat refers to as "purge": the stomach contents leaking out. Next she "fixes the features," setting them into a more dignified expression of repose before the chemicals go in and harden them into place. Make a face and someday it'll stay that way, your mother said: same principle at work here. To fix his jaw she threads a needle with twine, pops it through his upper palate and feeds the needle out through his nose and back again. Then, with some deft wrestling, it appears through a spot under his chin, and she pulls both ends taut until his head rises from the table. She saws the twine back and forth and ties it off over his teeth, and now his mouth is firmly shut. She tucks the ends of the twine under his lips, then plumps them lightly with one of her gloved fingers, and turns his head slightly to the right. In fact the textbook calls for exactly fifteen degrees of tilt, the proper "viewing position."

Then, the eyes. She uses plastic "eye-caps," little pink half-shell contacts, one side of which are pocked and nubby to keep the eye-lids in place, so they don't open up at an inopportune time, say, in the middle of an open-casket funeral. The corners of the eyes and mouth are droopy, so she applies some Dodge feature builder with a syringe, under the skin. Botox of death, she calls it. All the while she tells me about the renovations she and Robbie are doing at the house. They're painting the walls dark burgundy, and employing an African motif: monkeys and zebras and whatnot.

Just as I'm thinking we must be running out of things to do to the poor man, she cuts a hole above his right collarbone and uses forceps to fish out the common carotid artery and a heavy vein, snips them, and inserts a cannula attached to a rubber hose. The hose leads to a machine on the wall the size of an air conditioner. Into it she empties bottles of Permaglo, a tinting formaldehyde-based preservative, and Metaflow, red like cherry syrup, to break up clots and condition the blood vessels, and a water softener to take the hard edge off the mix. Machine on, she steps back, and the rubber hose hops on the man's chest.

Formaldehyde changes the structure of the body's protein, cooks it the way lime juice cooks seafood in a *ceviche*, making it inhospitable to the bacteria of decomposition. The man turns from yellow to patchy pink, as the blood runs free from the hole in his neck along a channel in the steel table, where it soaks my J Cloth and the sleeve of my scrubs, then empties into the toilet, where it'll be flushed into the Winnipeg sewage system and, as sometimes happens when the pumps at the North End Treatment Plant fail, into the Red River where, at Lockport, sport fishermen catch catfish for supper.

Nat claps her hands.

"Clots!" she says, watching the stream of blood. "I love clots! It means he's getting good distribution."

We massage his limbs and rub his feet and the palms of his hands with our knuckles, to encourage circulation, aware of the time on the clock over the door. In thirty minutes his family will be in the Committal Space for the viewing.

Natalie works with the speed and confidence of a professional athlete. She reads the body for color and tumescence as if she were reading an opposing team's defense.

She deems the distribution of chemical "not bad," except for his legs and feet, so she calls an audible: we'll open the two femoral arteries in the groin and pump in more chemical ("we"?). She feels for a spot on the fleshy inside of the man's right thigh and cuts a neat hole, tears back and forth at the tissue with her probe and forceps, then isolates the artery and ties it off with twine. She then passes me the knife and invites me to do the same on my side. I figure it's worth stopping here to consider my options. I'm all for learning by doing, but as a beginner I feel it's appropriate to plea-bargain my way down to a lesser duty: perhaps I can comb his eyebrows or rewash the hair on his chest until it's pillowy soft. Cutting a man open, even a dead one, strikes me as an act, like hang-gliding, that I'd rather read about than do. Behind her hazmat chador, I can see Nat blink, waiting me out.

"Only if you're comfortable," she says.

I do as I'm told.

I cut the skin, dig through muscle with my thumb. The hole is cold and wet and meaty. I find what might pass as a blood vessel and hook it with my forefinger.

"That's a nerve," Nat says.

I try again. In my peripheral vision I see the man wince, but of course it's just a trick of the air or my mind. I can feel my own groin tighten and I suspect I'll sit funny for a week. My thumb hooks another wet wormy thing.

"That's a muscle."

Third trip in, I come up with the plum, if only by the sheer process of elimination: the femoral artery, as thick as a penne noodle.

"Good," she says, and after snipping a hole in the vessel and pumping it with fluid from the cannula until his knees turn pink, she shows me how to close the incision with heavy twine in a baseball stitch, which is even harder than finding the artery because I can barely sew a shirt button, much less a hole in a human leg.

As I sew there's a knock at the door. It's Neil. This is less a spot check than a moment with the corpse, since as it happens he knows the man: they took Icelandic language lessons together. The dead man, Neil says, had a sense of humor, a cottage at a nearby lake and grandsons who play hockey. Except for the hum of the ventilation, the room is silent.

"Well," Nat says finally, "he has amazing drainage!"

Everyone smiles, because in the prep room good drainage is a valued quality, like good manners and good diction.

The last step calls for stabbing the man in the belly with a long steel harpoon called a trocar. Attached to a vacuum hose, the trocar sucks the fluids from the abdomen and heart and lungs, which will be replaced by more preservative. Nat has to stand on a kitchen stool to work the trocar, spearing it in and out, in a kind of ballet-fencing move, until the man's belly drops and he's dry, then she pours two bottles of purple Spectrum cavity fluid down the hose. When he's done chugging the Spectrum, she caps the hole in his abdomen with a plastic screw, paints his face and hands with Kalon cream, wraps him in a flannel sheet, and ships him to the dressing room, where he'll be suited and casketed and smudged with purple lipstick. I follow.

After dressing the bald man and winching him into a Prairie Beacon casket, we roll him on the "church truck," a casket dolly, into the Committal Space, where the light feels to dim after the fluorescents of the prep room, and my ears pop from the quiet. Nat leans in close enough to kiss the man, and blows gently on his face to clear away any errant powder. Then, as she lines up the casket under the pot lights, the gum falls out of her mouth and lands on the lid of the casket. She flicks it into the wastebasket and wipes the wood with her sleeve. As I follow her back stage again, I can see the family in the parking lot, two boys with wet hair and hockey jackets and a woman stamping her feet against the cold.

During the visitation, I stay in the back and study the Dodge chemical manual. If I'm to understand the odd amalgam of clinical science and spa treatment that makes up the prep room routine, I have to figure out my Permaglos from my Introfiants:

Permaglo: "Where it is important to create an illusion of vitality, the embalmer can rely on this classic arterial chemical to impart a stable, natural-looking glow to lifeless tissue."

Chromatech Pink: "Here are some of the comments of our testers: Doesn't fade, even after a week; very natural, I like it better than any other dye I've tried; excellent, a true pink; it didn't have any of the red tones, just the pink I wanted; more lifelike than other pinks."

Chromatech Tan: ". . . is especially well suited to people with somewhat darker complexions due to exposure to sun, ethnicity, etc."

Introfiant: "Treats low-protein, low-albumen, aged and 'institutional' cases with excellent response. . . . May be safely used on normal cases without risk of 'burning' or 'leatherizing.'"

The illusion of vitality—I know squat about Freud, I can't read him without getting dizzy, but somewhere he's described the uncanny, that powerful notion of fear in the face of the in-between: not real, not unreal, not human, but still kind of sort of. It's a paradox that Japanese robot makers have been trying to solve. They keep building human replicas that look more and more lifelike (usually, for some reason, like hot Japanese women), but as a result of a Promethean behavioral twist, they find that the closer they get to perfection the more frightening the end product appears. A mannequin is creepy, but in the right context (say, in a store window, not in your bedroom at night) it's not a source of fear. A cartoon character with human features is downright cute. But as you approach the point at which real and unreal are confused, the natural response is revulsion: roboticist Masahiro Mori called this the "uncanny valley." Wax figures and zombies and automata live in the valley. Embalmed corpses, too. Natalie says embalming delivers to mourners the opportunity to face up to death, to see it for real, and to know the person won't be coming back: the body is its own therapeutic tool for the balming of grief, a tool for transcendence. But explain that to my cognitive wiring. The embalmed corpse is an in-between: both a person and an object to fear.

Still, ours looked pretty good, now, I'll grant her that: all sleepy and peach-colored, his various holes and puckered stitchings well hidden under clothes.

My hands, meanwhile, are ice cold. It occurs to me I've been through a rite of passage, like a Bantu boy who kills his first antelope. The experience was thrilling, in a primitive way. I should probably bay at the moon tonight. In any case, having literally got my hands wet and my garment soaked in blood, there's not much doubt that I've been baptized as a make-believe undertaker.

Few of us have ever thought about the reality of embalming a dead body, let alone read about it. Here Jokinen uses humor to help make his narrative a bit less gruesome to his audience. Cite a specific passage or two where Jokinen tries to see the humor in his apprenticeship. How effective is this strategy?

Using Google or another search engine, search the web for information about how to train to become an undertaker. What kind of education is required? Are there schools, or programs in colleges and universities, one can attend? Are there any federal, state, or local requirements one must meet?

Former staff writer and Tokyo correspondent for Time magazine, Lisa Takeuchi Cullen was born and raised in Kobe, Japan. Her first novel, Pastors' Wives, is due out in June, 2013. The excerpt below, taken from her first book, Remember Me: A Lively Tour of the New American Way of Death describes how the ashes of a cremated person can be turned into real diamonds.

excerpt from

REMEMBER ME: A LIVELY TOUR OF THE NEW AMERICAN WAY OF DEATH

BY LISA TAKEUCHI CULLEN

ASHES TO ASHES, DUST TO DIAMONDS

How to Turn Your Loved One into Jewelry, and Why

A dog is yipping inside a well-kept brownstone in Manhattan's East Village. I climb the stairs to where a woman is waiting by an open door. "Come, come, Nica," says Peggy Atkinson to her Maltese, who jumps up against my legs and then skitters inside.

Peggy greets me politely, if guardedly. She is tiny, bespectacled, and dressed in a black turtleneck and long black skirt. She embodies my image of a Broadway voice teacher, which is what she is—all except for her voice, which is raspy with cold. It is our first meeting. We have spoken over the phone, and because I have asked, she is letting me witness an intensely personal event. Peggy Atkinson's husband is coming home today, and I am here to watch her open the package.

DON ATKINSON
1940-2004

Don Atkinson died in January 2004. His death was shockingly sudden; at sixty-three, he was as robust and blond and theatrically handsome as ever, until one night when his heart stopped working. He collapsed on the kitchen floor while getting an antacid pill at 4:00 a.m. The medics came, but Peggy knew it was no use.

After saying good-bye to his still-warm body at the hospital, Peggy had no desire to view it again. "What was Don was gone," she says simply. She had him cremated and for a while kept his ashes in a mahogany box atop her dresser. But she knew what she would do.

Not long ago, she had been reading a women's magazine—*Vogue*, or maybe it was *Better Homes & Gardens*—and had come across one of those little blurbs in the front section, this one about how they could make diamonds out of human cremated remains. Diamonds! She had shown the article to Don, and together they had exclaimed over the marvel of it. How perfect—how them. Whoever went first, they said, laughing, this was without question what the other would do.

After Don died, Peggy fished out that article. It listed a Chicago company called LifeGem, along with its Internet address. She looked it up and then telephoned. It would take eight ounces, the representative told her, gently— eight ounces of Don to make a gem.

"I didn't do it right away," she says. "I held back for a little while." Finally, with her brother's help, Peggy opened that heavy mahogany box. She cried then. "That was the hardest part, measuring and sending it. That was the hardest. Very emotional, opening up that sealed box."

Four months later, the diamond was ready. This morning at 9:00 a.m., the FedEx man delivered a box about the size of, but much lighter than, a dictionary. It is sitting here at the edge of her massive dining table.

Don and Peggy Atkinson were a classic New York actor couple. They met on the set of the original Broadway production of *Fiddler on the Roof,* Peggy cast as Chava, the younger, idealistic daughter who married the student Fyedka, played by Don. Peggy was twenty-five, a Brooklyn-born spitfire with Italian eyes and waist-length locks; Don, twenty-seven, was a muscular dancer from Ohio with yellow curls and a face-splitting grin. They met, fell in love, fought, broke up.

It was the apartment that brought them back together. "The Lower East Side was the Haight-Ashbury of New York in the 1960s" says Peggy—bohemian and slightly dangerous. Peggy walked up those stairs and saw an entire floor of a brownstone, an unbroken bowling alley of a space, high-ceilinged, room enough for two passionate people. She marched up to Don during the next show and handed him a note. "I've seen our apartment," it said. They met afterward at the Theater Bar on Forty-sixth Street, made up, moved in. They paid $150 a month to start. It would be home for the next thirty-five years.

This being an actor's home, photos, many of them professional, cover the mantels and bookshelves. There is a black-and-white head shot of Don, the kind actors bring on auditions with their résumés pasted on the back. He's over-the-top handsome, with a broad nose, lantern jaw, Chiclets teeth, and wide-spaced, narrow eyes, like a cartoon rendition of a prince. Here is the couple, sun-streaked and grinning, wearing yellow life jackets while swimming with the dolphins in the Bahamas. I like best the close-up of Don after a day of sailing the twenty-two-footer *Pegasey* they kept at Peggy's family house on Long Island, his beard and curls whitened by sea and salt, mischief in his smile.

This is not memory lane; these photos are fairly recent. This was their life just yesterday.

On the wall there is a poster-sized black-and-white portrait of the two of them on their wedding day. Peggy wears a cowl-neck sweater pulled over her head like a medieval headdress, and Don is in an Edwardian suit with ruffles. They look as though they have wandered off the set of *The Lion in Winter*. They held their medieval-themed wedding on the spectacular estate of a school for the deaf, with giant bowls of fruit and tables of pie. "Like Camelot," says Peggy.

Peggy didn't want a funeral for Don. No one who holds a medieval wedding would want a traditional hankiefest. She and Don's best friend, Ed, "designed and put together—no, that's not the right word—we *composed* the ceremony." The program was titled *A Celebration of the Life of Don Atkinson*. Don wasn't religious, but he had liked how he felt at the Marble Collegiate Church, so they held it there. Hundreds came. The show consisted of four scenes, each depicting stages of his adult life. Scene One: The Hoofer. Scene Two: The Director. Scene Three: The Salesman. Scene Four: The Man. Students sang "Seasons of Love," from *Rent*. Ed rewrote the lyrics to Stephen Sondeim's "Old Friends," from *Merrily We Roll Along*. Friends sang "Till There was

You" and "Try to Remember" and Handel's "Come unto Him." They closed with Elvis's "Blue Suede Shoes" and "Great Balls of Fire."

How many people hugged Peggy, she doesn't know. She does know she cried and cried.

The apartment is quiet now but for the bleating of a nearby car alarm. Peggy leads me through the place, which, like Don's funeral, is set up like a series of scenes in a play about their exquisitely eclectic lives.

SCENE ONE: The Actor. The scene is set, quirkily but charmingly, in the small bathroom off the kitchen. Its walls are plastered all the way to the ceiling with posters and playbills from all the shows they've done. Don could carry a tune, and Peggy could follow a step—"back then, you had to do everything"—but it was his athletic hoofing that led to his work with Jerome Robbins, Agnes de Mille, and Michael Kidd, and her arresting voice to her roles in *Two Gentlemen of Verona* and *Kismet*. In summers, they codirected the College Light Opera Company in Falmouth, Massachusetts. "We were," she says, "quite a team." But Broadway dancers have a shelf life, and when the calls began to dwindle, Don simply took up something else.

SCENE TWO: The Craftsman. Don loved woodworking, honing his skill building their bookcases and fireplace, and tried but failed to turn it into a business.

SCENE THREE: The Aficionado. Don loved wine and took a job at the famous neighborhood store Astor Wines and Spirits. He brought home bottles—"ruination" to Peggy's figure—and kept a log, over the years turning himself into an expert, particularly on the wines of Bordeaux, and earned the title of senior wine consultant.

SCENE FOUR: The Sportsman. Don loved to shoot, but the thought of killing animals made him nauseous. The mounted deer's head above the fireplace was retrieved from the trash. He named it Clarence and every Christmas hung its antlers with balls.

We have come to the grand piano. Peggy's second career is as voice teacher to a steady stream of students from New York University's Tisch School of the Arts. The open score on the stand is "Someone to Watch Over Me."

Peggy has cancer. She received the diagnosis the Christmas after she lost Don. She found an aggressive doctor and is battling the disease with a round of chemo. "I figure I have nothing to lose but my hair," she says, touching her ash blond wig. She smiles. "It's been a rough year."

She pauses, and our eyes rest on the FedEx box.

"Well," says Peggy, taking a deep, rattly breath. "Shall we?"

I saw a human diamond for the first time at the National Funeral Directors Association convention in Nashville.

LifeGem has an unassuming booth in a center aisle of the 108,000-square-foot convention expo, a couple of cloth-covered foldout tables with brochures—a far cry from the Vegas-style extravaganza over at the casket section. LifeGem's logo uses a quiet typeface for the company name, the dot over the "i" in the shape of a diamond with a crown of sparks over it. It's elegant and simple. In diamonds as in cremation, too much flash is ostentatious and disrespectful.

But the glass-enclosed case on a pedestal catches my eye. I park Mika's stroller to peer inside the case. There are five gems, one blue, the rest yellow. Some are cut in a round shape, some in an oval. The largest looks to be at least a carat.

A smiling man approaches. Greg Herro, LifeGem's CEO, is its public face and top salesman. He's the one they send to Japan and Australia and to talk to the press. Herro is one of four friends—two sets of brothers—from the Chicago area who have risked everything they own to launch a business selling diamonds made from cremains.

It all began with Rusty Vanden Biesen, who later on the phone describes for me what I would characterize as a lifelong death fetish. On visits to his grandparents' home in Germany, he says he grew obsessed with the numerous crucifixes that adorned the walls. He lay awake nights thinking about death symbols and what happens in the afterlife. He was five at the time.

The fixation continued into adolescence. "I would sit and think about death and dying, and I tried to comprehend infinite nonexistence," he says. "I was consumed with it." He was probably the first Goth in Oak Park, Illinois, and he didn't even know it.

All signs to the contrary, Vanden Biesen did not grow up to become a serial killer. Instead he became a corporate pilot. One day in 1999, he was trolling around the Internet when he came across a periodic table. It was then he experienced his eureka moment.

"I looked at the elements, and I realized diamonds are made from carbon, and people are made from carbon." The notion struck him: If the carbon could be extracted from human remains, could they be turned by artificial process into real diamonds?

The idea drove him mad with excitement. "I was going berserk, talking to everybody about this," he says. For Vanden Biesen, the prospect eased his fears of death: "It was a sense of relief that there is something, that I could be something other than buried or cremated and forgotten. Something that people would cherish and remember and keep, that my memory could continue to live."

Despite his utter lack of scientific expertise, Vanden Biesen, who has a bachelor's in business administration from Cardinal Stritch College in Milwaukee, threw himself into his pursuit. He read about lab-created diamonds, about applying high pressure under high temperatures to create seed crystals, the same process that would apply in nature but at warp speed. "In general terms, I was convinced this was something we could do," he says.

At this point in his story, I should say that I am finding all of this improbable. I have written about business for many years, and never have I heard such a fantastic start-up tale. It should not be this easy. I mean, I have noticed that my basset hound's drool has roughly the same properties as John Frieda Frizz-Ease Hair Serum, and you don't see me incorporating.

Vanden Biesen insists his ignorance was an asset. "A lot of people have so much knowledge that it's a barrier to discovering something new," he says. "I wasn't tainted that way. I didn't know I couldn't do it."

Of course, Vanden Biesen had help. "It was up to my partners to find a commercially viable way to do it." Vanden Biesen had gabbed about his grand idea to his brother, Dean, who is married to Greg Herro's wife's sister. Instead of laughing at him, the men and Greg's brother, Mike, began discussing the concept at family gatherings, at first abstractly, then with growing excitement. Rusty supplied the research; Dean, a production manager for a company that sells steel parts, had the manufacturing experience; Mike could set up the order and tracking process; Greg, a computer consultant and entrepreneur, knew how to start and run a business.

One by one, all quit their jobs and maxed out their credit cards. In October 2004, Rusty Vanden Biesen stopped flying planes. "I told my wife we may have to sell the house," he says.

Meanwhile, they had settled on a way to make diamonds out of cremains. Greg Herro explains the process to me.

The first step is to collect the cremains. Eight ounces of ashes can yield enough carbon to make up to ten diamonds of up to one carat each in size. Eight ounces is only a smidgen of the four to six pounds of ashes a human body produces—all of which is enough, the company says, for at least one hundred diamonds.

The ashes are mailed by the funeral home to the company in Chicago, where they are placed in what is called a crucible. I picture something religious and a little bit ominous, but it turns out to be a metal tube about eight inches in height and four inches in radius. (Crucible, when I bother to look it up, can mean a severe test or trial but also means "a vessel made of a refractory substance such as graphite or porcelain, used for melting and calcining materials at high temperatures.") The crucible is then sealed and etched with a sixteen-digit number used to track the gem's journey.

The second step, which LifeGem calls "purification," is the one in which they capture the carbon from the cremains. The capturing occurs in a factory outside of Pittsburgh, in an industrial-size oven set at roughly 3,500 degrees Celsius. It takes one month, at the end of which you're left with pure graphite from the carbon. It looks like pencil lead—shiny, silvery particles. "Beautiful, really," says Herro.

In the third stage, LifeGem "grows" the diamond. The pencil-lead graphite is placed in an industrial press, a square machine that's eight feet in height, width, and depth—about the size and shape of the back half of a Hummer. This machine presses down on the stuff from every direction at extremely high temperatures for anywhere from three to seven weeks. The longer the press time, the larger the diamond.

Once the press is opened, out comes a diamond in the rough, a dark yellow or blue hunk of rock candy.

It is in the fourth stage that the diamond appears. The rock candy is sent to cutters in Bismarck, Nebraska. This is interesting to me. I had not realized Bismarck had a thriving economy in diamond cutting. "I don't know, that's where the best guys we found are," says Herro. They need the best: Cutting diamonds made from cremains is very, very tricky. "They can crack," Herro says. "All diamonds can crack."

This, too, is interesting to me. I had not realized that diamonds, all diamonds, could crack; I had thought the diamond was the hardest substance on earth. I think about all the times I have whacked this little rock on my left ring finger on some unforgiving surface. As bad as I would feel cracking the stone my husband paid for by teaching fifty hours of clarinet lessons to fourth-graders, I think about how much worse I would feel if this stone were, say, my mom.

In order to ward against cracking and other problems, the cutter spends at least a month shaping and faceting the diamond. LifeGem's Web site says I can order my diamond in a round, princess, or radiant (a kind of rectangle) shape. If I have ordered a half-carat princess but they wind up with enough usable rock for a three-quarter-carat round, I can have that for no extra charge. Most folks choose the bigger rock.

Then, if I want, the cutter will laser-etch a message on the girdle, which is the fine edge around the abdomen of the diamond. No one can see the message without a loupe.

Finally, a certified gemologist from the Gemological Institute of America will check it out, labeling the rock an actual, honest-to-goodness diamond. This is a common misperception about LifeGem diamonds: Though the process to create them is artificial, the gem itself is not. The diamond receives a grade for size and brilliance, but not for color or clarity, given that only white diamonds receive those grades.

All LifeGem diamonds come in either yellow or blue. That was not necessarily by design—they just turned out that way—but LifeGem is trying to make the best of it, working hard to educate skeptical customers of the rarity and beauty of what are called, in industry parlance, "fancy" diamonds.

The yellow is intensely yellow with a spike of orange, like a cat's eye or a summer ale or, as the Web site says, "a sunset captured in time." The blue is prettier, in my opinion—like "a wave upon the ocean"—but costs twice as much because the process involves working with boron (a metalloid element) and takes some manipulation to achieve.

The result is breathtaking, as is the price. LifeGem charges $2500 to $14,000 for diamonds that range in size from a quarter to one full carat. "We hope to bring down the price as the technology improves," says Herro, sounding apologetic. Where once they hoped to see orders for one hundred diamonds a year, LifeGem now is making one hundred a month. I figure that amounts to a gross revenue of anywhere from $3 million to $16.8 million a year. I am thinking maybe Rusty Vanden Biesen is not so mental after all.

Back then, back in August 2002 when the company unveiled its product, all the world thought the whole thing was mental. WEIRD BUT TRUE! Shrieked the *New York Post*. The *Maryland Gazette* included LifeGem diamonds in its list of "Wild and Wacky" holiday gifts. HERE'S A WAY TO MAKE A LASTING IMPRESSION, sniggered the *Philadelphia Inquirer*. The *Orange County Register* called anyone who'd consider the process "looney-tooney survivors."

Imagine, then, being the first customer, the first person who couldn't care less if someone thought him looney-tooney, who felt this would be the best way to remember someone he loved very, very much. Imagine letting your loved one—no, *requesting* that she be the first human being ever turned into a diamond.

I couldn't. So I gave LifeGem's first customer a call.

VALERIE SEFTON
1974-2002
Bill Sefton is driving on an Illinois interstate when he takes my call. He owns a company in Chicago that processes credit card payments for banks, as well as a travel agency through which card owners can claim mileage. He travels to Chicago to conduct business, though his home is a five-acre ranch in Scottsdale, Arizona, where he lives with his wife, five horses, and forty vintage

muscle cars. The cars—Camaros, Corvettes, and Dodge Darts from the 1960s and 1970s—live in a 5,500-square-foot garage with a giant mural of an old-time Dodge dealership. He calls his home the Red 'Vette Ranch.

Bill is funny and easygoing in the manner of someone who is used to success. But even people who usually win occasionally lose, and it is not so long ago that Bill Sefton lost what he loved most.

Valerie, Bill's daughter, died at age twenty-seven in the summer of 2002. She was diagnosed with Hodgkin's disease soon after she had graduated from Northern Illinois University in DeKalb. Valerie had just been licensed to teach K–3 at an elementary school.

Over four and a half years, Valerie endured ten bouts of chemotherapy and two stem cell transplants. Before her last transplant, she wrote a letter to her family. She told them where the letter was and asked that they open it if she didn't make it.

The second transplant seemed to go well; doctors said it was technically a success. But the new immune system caused other complications, including viral encephalitis, a swelling of the brain.

In those last days, Valerie lost track of time and place, waking from trips to Australia and other places she'd never been, delighting over and over again at the news of her sister's second pregnancy, dipping her burger in chocolate pudding and pronouncing the taste "terrible."

In those last days, Bill camped out at his business partner's coach house in Naperville, traveling to and from the University of Chicago Hospital, logging fewer than twenty hours a week at work, sharing bedside vigil with his ex-wife, Valerie's mom. One morning he opened the *Chicago Tribune* to an article about LifeGem. "I thought, Wow, this is a perfect Val kind of thing. This would be a cool thing to do," he says. He longed to show Valerie, but by this time she did not know her surroundings. He tucked the article away and didn't mention it to anyone.

Bill left the hospital at 7:00 p.m. the night of September 10, 2002, satisfied that Valerie's condition seemed stable. His ex-wife, Chris, a registered nurse, was about to leave, too, when Valerie's blood pressure began to fluctuate. Chris called Bill at various points to update him on Valerie's condition. No one was very worried.

At 11:00 p.m., Valerie died.

In their devastation, the family found and read Valerie's last letter. In it, she explained—calmly, decisively, and very specifically—what she wanted done after her death.

She would have no viewing of her body. The steroids and chemo had left her swollen and bald, and no young woman wants to be remembered that way. She would allow in its place a memorial service displaying her beloved scrapbooks.

Valerie was especially clear about her remains. She was to be cremated. "But if you put me up on a mantel somewhere, I will come back and haunt you," she wrote. "Take my ashes, and break them up into small lots. Give them to my friends and my family. Have them put them where they'd like me to be."

After reading the letter, Bill went and fetched the article on LifeGem. He showed it to the family. "Everyone agreed," he says, "that it was exactly what she would have wanted."

Bill called LifeGem and ordered six stones: for himself; Valerie's mother, Chris; his wife, Becky; his sister, Kathy Rinna; Valerie's sister, Tracey; and Tracey's daughter, Emma. He recalled they cost him between $16,000 and $18,000—a small sum, he says, compared with the funeral and all the other death costs. The smallest diamond, for Emma, was 0.25 carat; the largest, his, measures 0.55. All are blue.

Greg Herro flew out to Scottsdale to deliver the diamonds himself. It was then that Bill learned of Valerie's place in history. He had agreed to media coverage of the diamond's delivery, and the intense attention made him ask Herro: "Valerie's got to be among the first, right?"

Bill says Herro looked nervous. "She *is* the first," said Herro.

"Wow!" How cool is that?" Bill says he responded. "My Valerie's the very first person ever turned into a diamond."

Imagine Herro's relief: LifeGem had lucked into a dream customer in Bill Sefton. He even gushes about the gem's imperfections. "It's unique because it's Valerie," he says. "The flaws in the stone give it a lot of fire and personality. That's Valerie, too. If I wanted a perfect stone, I'd go buy one."

Bill had his stone set into his wedding band, which he never removes. But the memorializing of Valerie Sefton did not end there. The diamonds fulfilled the spirit of Valerie's wishes, but the abundance of leftover ashes allowed the family to match the letter, too. The divvied them up in Ziploc bags. Her mother, Chris, found small wooden boxes with angels on top—Valerie had always loved angels—to act as mini-urns. Everywhere they went for the next few years, the angel boxes went, too. There's a little bit of Valerie in the waterfalls of Maui. There's some of her in Disneyland near a bronze statue of a little girl with a sea turtle (Valerie loved turtles). The workers at Bill's company took their box to her favorite place for lunch and left a little of her at the Cracker Barrel.

One portion of Valerie's ashes were set aside for Cori Ullman, her best friend. "You're a diamond in a pile of rocks," Valerie used to tell her. Cori couldn't afford a diamond, but swore she would someday. Last year, Cori got married. As a wedding gift, the Seftons gave Cori a canary yellow 0.6-carat diamond made of her best friend. She could not be the maid of honor, but Valerie was right there.

Bill is quiet for a moment. "Most times, when I think of her, I smile," he says, and his voice breaks, and he cries.

I picture this vibrant, generous man, driving alone down an Illinois highway, sobbing as he tells a stranger about the daughter he lost, the daughter who now sparkles from his left ring finger. It is not Valerie, but it is part of her, and that is something.

When he can speak again, Bill does not apologize for crying. He lost his girl. He can remember her however he damn well wants. He can cry before a stranger if he damn well wants. I am crying, too.

"We went through some real bad stuff for a real long time," he says. "There's not a lot of good stuff to remember. Every day I look at my ring. Every day I appreciate it. It's one of the most fulfilling things I've ever done."

SCENE FIVE: The Homecoming. In a high-ceilinged brownstone apartment in Manhattan's East Village, two women sit at a large, thick-legged dining room table. Between them on the table is a FedEx package, about the size of but much lighter than a dictionary. Peggy Atkinson, the woman dressed all in black sitting at the head of the table, nervously adjusts her glasses and smooths her ash blond wig. An expression of determination crosses her face. She takes a deep, rattly breath.

PEGGY: Well. Shall we? (Peggy, small and weakened by the cancer treatments, struggles with the box. The other woman, a journalist, takes it from her and carefully wrests open the gluey parts. There's a box inside a box, and then another box, like a Russian doll.)

PEGGY (murmurs): They don't make it easy, do they. (Finally they get to the bubble wrap, which surrounds a square black box about the size and weight of a drink coaster. Hands trembling, Peggy takes the package. It is a beautiful wooden jewelry box with a glass top. There, just under the glass on a velvety black surface, is Don—Don Atkinson, the diamond. The gem is round, the cut brilliant, the clarity high, the color bright yellow, the weight 0.5 carat.)

PEGGY (whispers): Oh, for God's sake, look at that. (Slowly, she opens the glass lid and rolls the gem gently into the palm of her hand.)

PEGGY: Oh, God. Isn't that beautiful? Look at it! (Suddenly she is consumed by the enormity of the moment. Here he is, her beloved husband, glinting up at her with all the sparkle and fire she remembered. Behind her glasses, her wide eyes brighten with tears.)

PEGGY: Oh, Donny. Donny. (When she speaks, she marvels in a steady, low voice about the wonder of the thing.) It's a half carat—all I could afford right now—but they said it came out a little bigger than that . . . I didn't know how the yellowing would turn out . . . have you seen others? Are they all as pretty as this? God, it's gorgeous . . . know what's engraved on it? "Shine on." That's what it says.

JOURNALIST: What will you do with it?

PEGGY: Oh, I've thought about it. Don designed our gold wedding bands. See—wavy, hand-chased. After his death I wore his on a chain around my neck, until it got too heavy—physically and emotionally. I'll go to one of

Don's jewelers. I'll ask him to make his wedding band and the diamond into a pendent. Then I'll wear it. Always. (She takes one long look before she returns the diamond to the box.)

PEGGY: I'm glad I did this. I know this is what he would have wanted. (She exhales, looks far away. Smiles. The moment is bittersweet.) I'd much rather have my husband, but . . .

Cullen chooses to explain through the use of narrative how a person's remains can be transformed into diamonds. She sandwiches the story of how the founders came up with the idea for the company between accounts of how two families chose to have diamonds made from the remains of a loved one. Why does Cullen choose to use narrative to explain this company? What does the reader gain from learning about the lives of two of LifeGem's customers?

Go to LifeGem's corporate Web site, http://www.irrproducts.com, and familiarize yourself with the products available, from the size, shape, weight, and cost of the diamonds, to the settings they can be placed within. Do you think the stones are attractive? Do you think the cost is reasonable? Explain.

Judging from Cullen's article, as well as the sales figures and testimonials found on LifeGem's Web site, many people find the idea of making a diamond out of the remains of a loved one a fitting tribute that's worth the cost. Do you agree? Would you consider paying to have the ashes from someone you loved made into one of these stones? Would you approve of someone doing the same with your ashes? Write a short essay—3 to 5 paragraphs—expressing your thoughts on this issue.

Journalist Jenna Wortham is a staff reporter for the New York Times, *where she specializes in Internet culture, social networking, and the interaction between culture and technology. Her work has also appeared in* Wired *magazine and* Wired Digital.

AS FACEBOOK USERS DIE, GHOSTS REACH OUT

BY JENNA WORTHAM

Courtney Purvin got a shock when she visited Facebook last month. The site was suggesting that she get back in touch with an old family friend who played piano at her wedding four years ago.

The friend had died in April.

"It kind of freaked me out a bit," she said. "It was like he was coming back from the dead."

Facebook, the world's biggest social network, knows a lot about its roughly 500 million members. Its software is quick to offer helpful nudges about things like imminent birthdays and friends you have not contacted in a while. But the company has had trouble automating the task of figuring out when one of its users has died.

That can lead to some disturbing or just plain weird moments for Facebook users as the site keeps on shuffling a dead friend through its social algorithms.

Facebook says it has been grappling with how to handle the ghosts in its machine but acknowledges that it has not found a good solution.

"It's a very sensitive topic," said Meredith Chin, a company spokeswoman, "and, of course, seeing deceased friends pop up can be painful." Given the site's size, "and people passing away every day, we're never going to be perfect at catching it," she added.

James E. Katz, a professor of communications at Rutgers University, said the company was experiencing "a coming-of-age problem."

"So many of Facebook's early users were young, and death was rare and unduly tragic," Mr. Katz said.

Now, people over 65 are adopting Facebook at a faster pace than any other age group, with 6.5 million signing up in May alone, three times as many as in May 2009, according to the research firm comScore. People over 65, of course, also have the country's highest mortality rate, so the problem is only going to get worse.

Tamu Townsend, a 37-year-old technical writer in Montreal, said she regularly received prompts to connect with acquaintances and friends who had died.

"Sometimes it's quite comforting when their faces show up," Ms. Townsend said. "But at some point it doesn't become comforting to see that. The service is telling you to reconnect with someone you can't. If it's someone that has passed away recently enough, it smarts."

Ms. Purvin, a 36-year-old teacher living in Plano, Tex., said that after she got over the initial jolt of seeing her friend's face, she was happy for the reminder.

"It made me start talking about him and thinking about him, so that was good," she said. "But it was definitely a little creepy."

Facebook's approach to the deaths of its users has evolved over time. Early on it would immediately erase the profile of anyone it learned had died.

Ms. Chin says Facebook now recognizes the importance of finding an appropriate way to preserve those pages as a place where the mourning process can be shared online.

Following the Virginia Tech shootings in 2007, members begged the company to allow them to commemorate the victims. Now member profiles can be "memorialized," or converted into tribute pages that are stripped of some personal information and no longer appear in search results. Grieving friends can still post messages on those pages.

Of course, the company still needs to determine whether a user is, in fact, dead. But with a ratio of roughly 350,000 members to every Facebook employee, the company must find ways to let its members and its computers do much of that work.

For a site the size of Facebook, automation is "key to social media success," said Josh Bernoff, an analyst at Forrester Research and co-author of "Groundswell: Winning in a World Transformed by Social Technologies."

"The way to make this work in cases where machines can't make decisions is to tap into the members," he said, pointing to Facebook's buttons that allow users to flag material they find inappropriate. "One way to automate the 'Is he dead' problem is to have a place where people can report it."

That's just what Facebook does. To memorialize a profile, a family member or friend must fill out a form on the site and provide proof of the death, like a link to an obituary or news article, which a staff member at Facebook will then review.

But this option is not well publicized, so many profiles of dead members never are converted to tribute pages. Those people continue to appear on other members' pages as friend suggestions, or in features like the "reconnect" box, which has been spooking the living since it was introduced last October.

Ms. Chin said Facebook was considering using software that would scan for repeated postings of phrases like "Rest in peace" or "I miss you" on a person's page and then dispatch a human to investigate that account.

"We are testing ways to implement software to address this," she said. "But we can't get it wrong. We have to do it correctly."

The scanning approach could invite pranks—as the notification form already has. A friend of Simon Thulbourn, a software engineer living in Germany, found an obituary that mentioned someone with a similar name and submitted it to Facebook last October as evidence that Mr. Thulbourn was dead. He was soon locked out of his own page.

"When I first 'died,' I went looking around Facebook's help pages, but alas, they don't seem to have a 'I'm not really dead, could I have my account back please?' section, so I opted for filling in every form on their Web site," Mr. Thulbourn said by e-mail.

When that didn't work, Mr. Thulbourn created a Web page and posted about it on Twitter until news of the mix-up began to spread on technology blogs and the company took notice. He received an apology from Facebook and got his account back.

The memorializing process has other quirks. Memorial profiles cannot add new friends, so if parents joined the site after a child died, they would not have permission to see all the messages and photos shared by the child's friends.

These are issues that Facebook no doubt wishes it could avoid entirely. But death, of course, is unavoidable, and so Facebook must find a way to integrate it into the social experience online.

"They don't want to be the bearer of bad tidings, but yet they are the keeper of those living memories," Mr. Katz, the Rutgers professor, said. "That's a real downer for a company that wants to be known for social connections and good news."

According to Wortham, death is a fact of life that social networking sites, as well as other online entities, must find a way to account for in their online structure. What options does Wortham discuss in the article? What problems does she identify? What do you think should happen when a user of a site like Facebook dies?

Choose a social networking site you frequent—or some other online site, such as Yahoo or an online gaming site—and find out what kind of policies the site has established (if any) regarding the death of a user. Does the site have a way to memorialize a user? Can family or friends access the site after someone dies?

Guy Trebay writes for the New York Times, *where he covers fashion and style. His work has also appeared in such publications as the* New Yorker, *the* Village Voice, *and* Harper's *magazine.*

LOST TO AIDS, BUT STILL FRIENDED

By Guy Trebay

Like millions of other Americans, Dominic Bash has a Twitter account, an online wall and a network of friends on the Web. His Facebook-style profile features Mr. Bash's occupation as a hairdresser at the Abbey in Philadelphia, lists his birthday, the names of good friends, his interests and hobbies. It pictures him at his most typical and outrageous—at a Philadelphia gay pride parade, dressed in a lavender feather boa, his long blond hair styled in a braid reminiscent of Madonna, in her Heidi phase.

Mr. Bash's profile also contains information less customary on social networking sites: the date of his death. Mr. Bash, 46 when he died in 1993, was a member of what a friend refers to as a lost generation of gay men, among the many who died of AIDS before the development of antiretroviral drugs rendered H.I.V. treatable.

"There is a real hunger for information about this period, this history and these lost lives," said that friend, Chris Bartlett, a former classics scholar who has set out to rescue the memories of those lives, specifically 4,600 gay Philadelphia men who perished of AIDS in the 1980s and '90s. While the memorializing impulse is ancient, the method Mr. Bartlett came up with is as new as the latest app; he has created a social networking site for the dead.

Modest by the standards of memorial Web sites like Tributes.com—a for-profit company that amasses 80 million obituaries—Mr. Bartlett's site, gayhistory. wikispaces.com, is far from the first AIDS commemoration. But its appearance now links it to a resurgence of attempts to reclaim the memories of thousands who died during a calamitous era, when H.I.V. was still a death sentence. It connects the dead to one another, to a larger community and to groups of potential new "friends" using technology that most of those it commemorates did not live to experience.

"There is absolutely no permanent social marker of the hundreds of thousands who died of AIDS in this country," said Sarah Schulman, a writer and a director of the Act Up Oral History Project, begun seven years ago to assemble testimonies from the surviving members of the activist group AIDS Coalition to Unleash Power.

"There's not even a postage stamp."

That is in part why the Carpenter Center for the Visual Arts at Harvard opened an exhibition in October of agitprop produced by the New York chapter of Act Up between 1987 and 1993, years when AIDS fatalities in the United States climbed, with grim inexorableness, to a 1995 peak of over 51,000, according to the Centers for Disease Control and Prevention.

"I was shocked when I came to Harvard to discover that no one remembered Act Up," said Helen Molesworth, the show's curator. "The defining political movement of my generation was not known at all by people 15 years younger than myself, and that absence of knowledge seemed quite horrible to me."

The ignorance is a result in part of the success of antiretroviral drugs in rendering AIDS a manageable disease. What Ms. Schulman termed the "naturalization" of AIDS occurred as generations indoctrinated with lessons of abstinence and safer sex practice lost touch with a time when AIDS was stigmatized as a "gay plague." To a contemporary 25-year-old, it might seem improbable that there was ever an era when New Yorkers in the prime of their lives habitually turned to the obituaries before reading the headline news.

When filming "Last Address," a new short film that will have its debut at the Sundance Film Festival in January, the director Ira Sachs focused on the residences of a handful of creative New Yorkers (the photographers Peter Hujar and Robert Mapplethorpe, the poet Cookie Mueller, the playwright Charles Ludlam) who were among the tens of thousands in the city lost to AIDS.

It was his way, Mr. Sachs said, "of recognizing absences but also the presence of this entire generation that died in one fell swoop."

A similar impulse went into the creation of "Persistent Voices: Poetry by Writers Lost to AIDS," an anthology published this month in an effort to revive the memories and careers of gay poets like Tim Dlugos, Joe Brainard and Gil Cuadros, whose posthumous reputations dwindled as their work became increasingly obscure.

"These writers were all living, writing and dying before my gay consciousness was formed," said Philip Clark, 29, an editor of the anthology. "Lots of these poets did not have wide readerships during their lives. And most of them died when the Internet was in its infancy."

It was online that Mr. Clark researched the lives of men like Essex Hemphill, a Philadelphia-based poet who is, as it happens, one of the members of Mr. Bartlett's social network. "The Internet gives us this giant opportunity to save these people and to start a dialogue about what has been lost and forgotten and to stop that loss," Mr. Clark said.

With its generic graphics and simple links, the Philadelphia-area social network of the dead, called The Gay History Wiki, lacks the jaunty bulletin-board appeal of Facebook or MySpace. "A social network for the dead shouldn't be too fancy," said its creator, Mr. Bartlett. But neither, he added, should it be too spooky or grim. Like the AIDS quilt, a celebrated multiyear project to commemorate and document the AIDS pandemic, one quilt panel at a time, the site was forced into existence to commemorate people whose lives risked being forgotten, but also as a means of assembling in one place the random fragments of an atomized community and carrying its stories into the future.

"So much was lost when those lives were ripped out of the heart of the city," said Mr. Bartlett. "There were 4,600 men who died from a gay male population of about 26,000" in Philadelphia, he added. When men like Mr. Bash, the hairdresser, who was also a fierce and early AIDS treatment advocate, died, they took with them a crucial piece of recent cultural history. The controversial nun Sister Jeannine Gramick, whose ministry to lesbian and gay Catholics eventually led to a Vatican inquiry, has credited Mr. Bash as an early inspiration for her activism.

"There are a lot of stories like that," said Mr. Bartlett. "Also a lot of stories of ordinary Joes."

Beginning in 2005, Mr. Bartlett began assembling the names of every gay male Philadelphian who died after being diagnosed with H.I.V. or AIDS, searching obituaries and the Names Project registry of people commemorated by the AIDS quilt, combing through records of social clubs and the rosters at St. Luke and the Epiphany, the Philadelphia church that took on the task at the epidemic's height of "burying the people no one else would," Mr. Bartlett said.

Inspired by Steven Spielberg's Shoah project, a Holocaust memorial, in 2007 Mr. Bartlett built a database on wikispaces.com, the free portal that invites editorial interventions, and by the end of last summer was ready to broadly promote his site. Unlike the AIDS quilt, an intensely elegiac but largely static artifact, the Gay History Wiki is a sprightly free space open to posts and tags, to biographical data added and amended by survivors for their vanished friends.

While Facebook's "memorialization" mode, which provides for the maintenance of accounts in the names of the dead, limits access to those who were listed as friends at the date of death, Mr. Bartlett's site is, in customary wiki style, open to all.

Beyond the novelty of this approach is something equally important, Ms. Schulman of the Act Up Oral History Project suggested: the opportunity to fill in blanks in a haphazard narrative. "The AIDS story has been limited to depictions of doomed individuals," and not impassioned, ad hoc communities, she said.

A conviction that gay men and women and their friends came to one another's assistance during the crisis—improvising buddy systems, treatment groups, food banks and other survival networks—fueled Mr. Bartlett's pursuit, as he recreated a mesh of lives that unexpectedly turned out to have meaning for a cohort of young gay men.

"Everyone knows AIDS is a big issue, but for people 25 and under, it's not really a topic of discussion," said Evan Urbania, a 29-year-old marketer who regularly visits the Gay History Wiki. "I'm a social media guy, and the importance of involving the stories of people who have passed on, particularly as a gay man whose development was influenced by people who are 20 or 30 years older, is very powerful to me."

Online stories told by men of an earlier generation motivated Mr. Urbania to take up volunteer work in the AIDS-care community. "One guy told stories of smuggling AZT from Mexico to the U.S., when it was unavailable," he said, referring to an early AIDS drug. "He was going over the border to bring it back. It becomes a huge problem for us as a generation if we forget these experiences that shaped and guided what it is to be gay today"

Thus far, concerns about the ethics of linking random strangers under the rubric of a still-stigmatized disease have failed to materialize. But a few others have raised questions about the site.

"The positive side of this effort seems to be to bring the lost back into the community of the living and to honor them," said the Rev. Paul Raushenbush, associate dean of religious life at Princeton University, who is gay. "However, it is one thing to be remembered and another to be recreated. Does it honor their lives to bequeath their personalities to a two-dimensional characterization on the Internet?"

Memorials, as Mr. Bartlett noted, are for the living, of course, and not the dead. Particularly when it comes to recent gay history, he said, the imperative to document a moment that risks being lost outweighs other concerns.

"At this point, everybody knows the value of participating in a social network that's alive," said Mr. Bartlett, who is linked as a friend of Dominic Bash online and whose Twitter address is the name of another gay man who is long gone: @Harveymilk. "I'm making the case that the value people offer to a social network does not disappear when they die," he said.

Trebay argues that "the value people offer to a social network does not disappear when they die." What do you think about establishing profiles of the dead on social media sites such as Facebook, or on individual databases sites such as wikispaces.com?

Go to http://www.respectance.com, an online tribute and memorial Web site where subscribers can establish memorial pages for friends and family members who have died. Click on a few such pages and examine what images and texts are included as a tribute to the dead. Do you share the concern raised by Rev. Paul Raushenbush in this article that such online memorials reduce the dead to a "two-dimensional characterization on the Internet?" Would you want to be remembered in this way after you die?

Jessica Moore is a working mother and wife, and a part-time member of the Air National Guard. She is a veteran of the United States Air Force and deployed in support of Operation Enduring Freedom. She uses writing to help her cope with tough times in her life, including this blog post describing her grief over losing a close friend.

DEATH IS ONLY A HORIZON

BY JESSICA MOORE

Jeremiah and I shared similar political views and we created a friendship based on mutual admiration of each other's talents. He was an excellent writer and he would sometimes ask me to proofread his pieces; I also enjoy writing and I would sometimes compose things based on his suggestions. We both loved music and I would invite him to hang out with me at karaoke bars. He was always encouraging and would suggest songs for me to sing when I got tired of my regular repertoire. He particularly liked it when I would sing "Crimson and Clover."

He was a very intriguing character. He wrote under a pseudonym and that was the name he used on his social networking pages. He was tattooed and pierced and told stories of times that he'd been stabbed or been involved in biker fights. But he was a sweet and tender father to his daughter. Halloween was his favorite holiday, second only to his birthday, which he thought should be a nationally celebrated event. He was possibly atheist, but at least agnostic. His writing and musical tastes ran to dark fantasy and death metal, but he could pull off a great George Thorogood and loved to sing Violent Femmes. We also shared an unlikely love of They Might Be Giants.

I planned his thirtieth birthday party and it was a huge success. I remember when his mother died and I listened for hours as he told me all about her and how wonderful she was. When I went through a bad breakup Jeremiah would come to the bar and, when I started getting a little too drunk, he would walk me home. He made sure I got in the house and locked the door behind me. He was the only one who showed up to help me when I moved. When I fell in love with my husband and we got married in Vegas, Jeremiah was very happy for us and helped me find a place to have a local ceremony.

Jeremiah and I both held a deep respect for beauty. He would share with me pictures he took or text me to say "Look at the moon!" I enjoyed being one of his friends and I knew I could count on him for anything. He got a new job and also was granted primary custody of his daughter, so our nights out diminished and so did our communication with one another.

The last time I saw Jeremiah was at a karaoke bar, not surprisingly. I can't really remember when it was, but it was cold out. We had a great time and I hugged him when I left and told him that I loved him. He said he loved me, too.

In November of last year, I got a message from someone I didn't know on Facebook that said, "I'm a friend of Jeremiah's. One of the last conversations we had he mentioned you. You were special to him so I wanted to make sure you knew that he'd passed away." He listed his phone number and I texted him right away to say I didn't think his joke was very fucking funny. Jeremiah was only 34, there was no way he could be dead. He called me right away and told me he wasn't joking, but he really wished he was. Jeremiah had died of a heart attack.

I was in my car at the time and pulled over to cry. My 12 year old son was with me and he tried to comfort me. I spent the next few days watching his Facebook page for details about services. I read in a book when I was younger that you should always try to touch the person because it will help you heal. I touched Jeremiah's hand when we arrived at the funeral and I wish against wish I hadn't. It was hard and felt like wax; nothing like the warm hand that would squeeze my shoulder when I had a particularly difficult customer on the line.

The church was packed for the service and it was very religious, considering Jeremiah's beliefs . . . or lack thereof, as the case may be. Afterwards, the preacher invited all of Jeremiah's friends to come forward and be saved from our sinful ways. I thought it was tacky and offensive for them to imply that anyone who wasn't a Christian wouldn't see Jeremiah on the other side, or whatever version of afterlife they believe in. But they did play a few songs that Jeremiah requested be played in this situation—of course he had already planned for this—and they gave us two poems he had written, one for his mother and one for his father.

I watched his Facebook page daily for a while. It's been taken down now, and I miss that connection. A lot of us would post random memories or pieces of his writing as we found them. One friend said he found, in his phone, an ominous text reply from the night before Jeremiah died. The friend had asked "Are you there yet?" And Jeremiah said, "I'm always somewhere."

Jessica Moore is a blogger with a long-established and popular blog. Here, she relates finding out about the death of a friend via Facebook. Given Wortham and Trebay's views on death and social media, what do you think about Moore's experience? Are social media sites a boon to people when it comes to the death of a loved one, or an intrusion?

DEATH

Born in the UK, journalist Sarah Murray writes about the relationship between business and society. Her recent book, Making an Exit: From the Magnificent to the Macabre—How We Dignify the Dead, was published in 2011 by St. Martin's Press.

WHEN MOURNING GOES VIRAL

By Sarah Murray

THE 2.5 MILLION TWEETS AFTER STEVE JOBS' DEATH PROVE JUST HOW PROFOUNDLY SOCIAL MEDIA HAVE TRANSFORMED MOURNING.

Soon after news of Steve Jobs' death emerged Wednesday, millions of hashtags, posts and YouTube videos erupted on Facebook and Twitter to memorialize his life and express sadness for the loss of a technology visionary. Twitter alone was overrun with 2.5 million tweets about Jobs in the 12 hours after he died. As someone who revolutionized the digital world, it seems eminently appropriate that mourners took their grieving online—especially since social media has, in many ways, helped reinvent the way we approach death in modern society.

First, it gives people who have something to say an unprecedented audience that's both instantaneous and quintessentially democratic. The eulogy is no longer the preserve of the great and the good. Online, anyone can be a broadcaster, a commentator or a curator of news and information.

Social media has also awakened the newshound in many of us. We want to be the first to comment, and when it comes to death, we no longer have to sit back passively and wait for the obit in the next morning's newspaper. Moreover, we can be part of a popularity contest, as blogs listing the "10 most quoted tweets about Steve Jobs" demonstrate.

Using death as a competition to produce the fastest tweet or the post with the most hits might seem a little self-serving and, frankly, insensitive. But there's more to this than just a race to be first. Collective mourning is important in any society. It unites us and gives us permission to contemplate personal loss—to pull those deep reserves of grief out from their hiding places. Social media assists this process. More of us can engage when, rather than having to walk to a remembrance site (or an Apple store) with a yellow ribbon or drive to a roadside shrine with flowers, we can sit at home and tap out our feelings.

When it comes to grieving, social media gives us instant, global connectivity as well as a rich palette for expression. Online, text, photographs, audio and video mean we can easily share memories and broadcast public reflection. Essentially, technology is turbo-charging the process of collective mourning.

However, social media also returns to us things we've lost—a few rules, for a start. Today's secular society gives little guidance on how to deal with grief. In the absence of traditional mourning rituals, we struggle in the face of death. What should we say? What should we do? In societies where ritual remains strong, no one needs to ask how to express loss or honor the dead. Specified times and places for grieving are part of carefully defined cultural conventions. The rules allow for emotion but set boundaries for mourners, preventing unfettered anguish from being let loose.

If rituals provide ways of containing our grief, online formats do something similar. They give us room for creativity but they also set limitations (in the case of Twitter, that's 140 characters). Whether it's Facebook's wall, an online newsfeed or a tweet, online formats establish the kinds of frameworks that help us hold it together when we feel we're falling apart.

Technology also gives us back convening power. For death has never—at least until recently—been a solitary affair. You still see it in the Jewish tradition of sitting Shiva, with friends and neighbours visiting the bereaved during the seven-day mourning period. In New Guinea, the moment someone from the Mafulu tribe of dies, all the men start shouting loudly—or at least they did in 1910, when ethnologist Robert Wood Williamson, recorded details of their death rites. This was partly to scare off evil spirits, but as the chain of shouts moved from village to village, residents from surrounding valleys poured into the home of the deceased as word spread that the community had just lost one of its members.

Obviously, this isn't so easy today. Friends and family are dispersed more widely than ever. In this globalized world, we need to find ways of shouting about our dead and places in which to gather to express empathy and support. And if we can't do that physically, we can do it online. As humans, we're hardwired to form communities and to unite at our most significant moments. So while in volume, speed and global reach, what we saw on Wednesday in the wake of Steve Jobs' death was new, in some ways it was nothing more than a high-tech version of a practice that's been going on for centuries—the practice of getting together to say goodbye.

Murray uses the death of Steve Jobs to list a number of benefits social media provides for mourning, both individually and collectively. Identify three main benefits social media provides to society in terms of mourning. Do you agree or disagree with her claims? Explain.

Death

Former Baghdad Bureau Chief for Newsweek, *journalist Rod Nordland currently writes for the* New York Times.

HOW GRIM WAS MY VALLEY

By Rod Nordland

A TEEN SUICIDE EPIDEMIC SWEEPS A COMMUNITY IN WALES.

The string of deaths began with Dale Crole, 18. He hanged himself at an abandoned warehouse on Jan. 5, 2007. His friend David Dilling, 19, took police to the scene. Dilling died the same way a few weeks later, in mid-February. A week later the boys' friend Thomas Davies, 20, hanged himself in a local park. After two months' respite another local youth, 21-year-old Alan Price, was found dead of similar causes. In June his friend Leigh Jenkins, 22, hanged himself in another friend's bedroom. Another of Crole's friends, Liam Clarke, 20, died the same way in a park two days after Christmas. An acquaintance of his, Gareth Morgan, 27, hanged himself at home on the anniversary of Crole's death.

The people of Bridgend are baffled and scared. Since the start of 2007, a total of 17 young people in and around the played-out South Wales coal town—most of them teenagers—have killed themselves by hanging. Few townspeople had any idea at first that the deaths were something out of the ordinary. The suicide rate in Wales is nearly twice that of the United Kingdom as a whole, and sinkholes of poverty like Bridgend tend to be even worse. In the town and its surrounding valleys, an area with a total population of some 130,000, the suicide rate among males 15–24 over the past decade has been 43 per 100,000, more than double the Welsh rate of 19 per 100,000. But Bridgend has never suffered so many suicides in such quick succession—particularly among so many who were friends or acquaintances. And no one knows why it's happening now.

The deaths have accelerated in recent weeks. Each new suicide has inspired another memorial page on popular social-networking Web sites like Bebo. Natasha Randall, 17, posted a cheery tribute on Liam Clarke's memorial page on Jan. 15: "RIP Clarky boy!! gonna miss ya! Always remember the gd times!" Two days later she hanged herself. And that was another odd thing: doctors say women rarely ever commit suicide that way; they're far more likely to take pills or slit their wrists. Even so, the next day one of Randall's girlfriends tried to hang herself; luckily found by her father, who cut her down in time to save her life. A third young woman, 18-year-old Angeline Fuller, did hang herself two weeks later. Then came the deadliest five days yet: Nathaniel Pritchard, 15, hanged himself on Feb. 15, followed a few hours later by his 20-year-old cousin and neighbor, Kelly Stephenson, an accomplished athlete. Four days later their 16-year-old neighbor Jenna Parry, a trainee hairdresser, who was found hanging from a tree near her home on the city's outskirts.

Britain's tabloids went wild, with Fleet Street headlines like DEATH VALLEYS and SUICIDE TOWN and free-floating speculation of an Internet-spawned suicide pact. Local officials responded with righteous fury, denouncing the press for its insensitivity and suggesting that the barrage of media attention had encouraged more suicide attempts. "What's the link since Natasha Randall's death?" said assistant chief constable David Morris at a press conference. "It is you—the media!" Some townspeople viewed the situation differently. "I don't think they should blame the media," says Bridgend resident Tracy Roberts. "The media have at least highlighted the problem that they're not putting the services into these dead-end towns where we have to live." Her 19-year-old son, Anthony Martin, hanged himself in Bridgend last April, although he evidently had no ties to the other victims. Arthur Cassidy, a social-psychology professor who runs a youth-suicide intervention group in Belfast, agrees that the deaths aren't the tabloids' fault. "We have no evidence that newspapers influence suicidal behavior," he says. "Young people don't read newspapers. They get their news on the Internet."

The Internet is a recurring theme in the Bridgend hangings. Most and possibly all of the victims were members of the Bebo networking site, and many of them posted messages on the public memorial pages of those who preceded them in suicide. "I'm sure they all knew each other," says Ferdinand, 14, who lives near the 17th victim's house. (The boy's last name is withheld at his father's request.) "I knew six of them myself," the boy says. "I've been on some of their personal pages on Bebo, and they were talking about 'I don't think I can cope with it,' and 'I'm going to end it.' I didn't think they'd really do it." His friend George adds, "It's like it's the fashion or something."

According to Frederick and other kids in the area, local cops are visiting the homes of young people who have posted possibly suicidal messages on Bebo, and the site has been taking down those postings. Bebo spokesman Sam Evans, replying by e-mail to *Newsweek's* queries, confirmed that Bebo does remove profile or memorial pages of deceased persons upon requests by family members or law enforcement. "Bebo is working with South Wales police to assist with the ongoing investigation in any way it can," says Evans.

Police are still looking into the deaths, Morris said last week. He was emphatic on one point in particular: "I would like to put to bed at this moment any suggestion that we are investigating suicide pacts or suicide Internet links." Tabloid hype aside, Professor Cassidy urges special attention to suggestions that online connection is worth a close look. He cites research demonstrating that "suicide clusters" like the one in Bridgend nearly always result from some sort of "conscious form of agreement" among the victims—even if they have only the loosest personal connections to one another, as is common on social-network sites.

Others in the prevention field agree that suicide can spread like a virus over the Internet. "These social-networking sites, especially ones that deal with young people, have a responsibility to police their sites that they're not always fulfilling," says Paul Kelly of Papyrus, a teen-suicide prevention group in the United Kingdom. "There is a danger of glorifying young people who have taken their own lives."

Still, there are Internet operators who take such fears seriously. The obituary Web site GoneTooSoon.co.uk removed all tributes to the Bridgend victims last week, replacing them with its apologies and an explanation. The site's founder, Terry George, says he wants to avoid any possibility of glamorizing the deaths. "If you commit suicide in the hope you'll be well-known afterwards, then it won't happen with us," he says. "We won't allow it. Something has to be done to stop these people taking their own lives." Bebo's approach has been less dogmatic. As recently as last Wednesday, Feb. 27, the site included memorial pages for Nathaniel Pritchard and Jenna Parry, as well as a group page called Bridgend Deaths with hundreds of members, most of them young people. Their commentary ranged from the sentimental ("Hope you're all happy up there") to the crude.

A shocking array of resources for would-be suicides is readily available on the Web. Some sites promote euthanasia for the elderly or terminally ill, while others are explicitly aimed at troubled young people. One such site, registered to an address in Amsterdam, hosts a discussion on the most effective way for a minor to commit suicide, with posts ranging from crude and humorous to instructive and practical. The site's moderator, who portrays himself as a defender of "freedom of speech on the subject of suicide," nevertheless admits he has no qualifications, medical or otherwise, for providing advice to would-be suicides. "I don't think 'psychological professionals' are the only ones who should deal with the subject," he told *Newsweek* via e-mail.

Bridgend's people could tell him a few things about the pain and damage that suicide inflicts on the victim's survivors. Local authorities are promising to unveil a "suicide action plan" soon, and legislators in Wales have declared the goal of reducing suicides by 10 percent there this year. At this point, though, the most visible response to the Bridgend epidemic has come from volunteer groups such as the Samaritans, a British group that specializes in suicide counseling and runs hotlines at 200 branches across the country. The Bridgend chapter alone takes 30,000 calls a year. At night the group's volunteers fan out into the streets, waging a youth-oriented campaign with posters declaring I FEEL LIKE #!*%. More needs to be done, says Bridgend branch director Darren Matthews; some local schools aren't even discussing the problem with their students.

Such silence can be fatal. Early on the morning of Feb. 19 the body of the 17th victim, Jenna Parry, was found hanging from a leafless little tree at the edge of a village common, a popular gathering place for local kids who call it the Snake Pit. Several homes can be seen a couple hundred yards away, across a field. The branch she used was barely high enough to keep her feet off the ground. Last week the tree was festooned with dozens of messages, flowers and butterfly knickknacks, including a purple wind chime of glass butterflies. (Friends and family sometimes called her Butterfly). "Save me a place with you," said one unsigned note. Similar thoughts were posted on Parry's RIP page on Bebo. "Your In A Better Place Now!" wrote a friend with the online name Sexyyjodi. "i'll See You Soon! LoveYouuSooMuchhh!!" Parry's friends can only wonder why their love failed to save her life and why others seem open to the same tragic fate.

Nordland's article is a chilling account of a series of teenage suicides in a town in Wales seemingly linked only by the social networking site, Bebo. If these teens really did commit suicide because they were influenced by others on Bebo, what Nordland calls a "conscious form of agreement," what does this imply about the danger of social networking for teens?

Bebo is a social networking site, much like Facebook, begun in 2005 by Michael Birch. Go to http://www.bebo.com and examine the site. How is it like Facebook? How is it different from Facebook? If you Google "social-networking sites" how many other such sites appear? Are there any reviews of these sites on the Internet? Do some cater more to teenagers and some more to adults? Explain.

DEATH

NOTE TO SELF: YOU CAN'T CHEAT DEATH

By Ryan Hudson

DEATH

Native American leader, military commander of the Shawnee, and creator of the large tribal alliance known as Tecumseh's Confederacy, Tecumseh was born in what is now the state of Ohio in 1768. He grew up during the American Revolutionary War, later joining with the British against America during the War of 1812. He took part in the capture of Fort Detroit and was later killed in the Battle of Thames in 1813. He is honored in Canada as a hero whose military leadership helped the British keep the Americans out of Canada during the War of 1812.

ATTITUDE TOWARD DEATH

BY TECUMSEH, CHIEF OF THE SHAWNEE

Live your life that the fear of death

can never enter your heart.

Trouble no one about his religion.

Respect others in their views

and demand that they respect yours.

Love your life, perfect your life,

beautify all things in your life.

Seek to make your life long

and of service to your people.

Prepare a noble death song for the day

when you go over the great divide.

Always give a word or sign of salute when meeting or

passing a friend, or even a stranger, if in a lonely place.

Show respect to all people, but grovel to none.

When you rise in the morning, give thanks for the light,

for your life, for your strength.

Give thanks for your food and for the joy of living.

If you see no reason to give thanks,

the fault lies in yourself.

Touch not the poisonous firewater that makes wise

ones turn to fools and robs the spirit of its vision.

When your time comes to die, be not like those

whose hearts are filled with fear of death,

so that when their time comes they weep and

pray for a little more time to live their lives over

again in a different way.

Sing your death song, and die like a hero going home.

Using your campus or local library, or an Internet search engine such as Google or Bing, do some research in order to learn more about the life of Chief Tecumseh. When did he live? What role did he play historically?

As you read Chief Tecumseh's speech, what kind of attitude toward death does the speaker portray? Do you agree or disagree with his view of death?

In a short essay (2 to 3 paragraphs), compare the speaker in this speech to the speaker in Blue Öyster Cult's song lyric, "(Don't Fear) The Reaper," on page 5. How are their views of death alike? Different? Be sure to use specific passages from each text to support your claims.

DEATH

British author and playwright A. A. Milne is most famous for his 1928 creation of Winnie-the-Pooh. The boy in the Pooh novels, Christopher Robin, was modeled after Milne's own son of the same name, while the other characters were all fashioned after his son's stuffed animals, including his bear, Winnie-the-Pooh, named after a real Canadian bear left to the London Zoo after WWI. After Milne's death, his heirs sold their rights to the Pooh books to Disney for more than 350 million dollars.

excerpt from
THE HOUSE AT POOH CORNER

BY A.A. MILNE

Then, suddenly again, Christopher Robin, who was still looking at the world with his chin in his hands, called out "Pooh!"

"Yes?" said Pooh.

"When I'm—when—Pooh!"

"Yes, Christopher Robin?"

"I'm not going to do Nothing any more."

"Never again?"

"Well, not so much. They don't let you."

Pooh waited for him to go on, but he was silent again.

"Yes, Christopher Robin?" said Pooh helpfully.

"Pooh, when I'm—*you* know—when I'm *not* doing Nothing, will you come up here sometimes?"

"Just Me?"

"Yes, Pooh."

"Will you be here too?"

"Yes, Pooh, I will be *really*, I *promise* I will be, Pooh."

"That's good," said Pooh.

"Pooh, *promise* you won't forget about me, ever. Not even when I'm a hundred.'

Pooh thought for a little.

"How old shall *I* be then?"

"Ninety-nine."

Pooh nodded.

"I promise," he said.

Still with his eyes on the world Christopher Robin put out a hand and felt for Pooh's paw.

"Pooh," said Christopher Robin earnestly, "if I—if I'm not quite—" he stopped and tried again—"Pooh, *whatever* happens, you *will* understand, won't you?"

"Understand what?"

"Oh, nothing." He laughed and jumped to his feet.

"Come on!"

"Where?" said Pooh.

"Anywhere," said Christopher Robin.

So they went off together. But wherever they go, and whatever happens to them on the way, in that enchanted place on the top of the Forest, a little boy and his Bear will always be playing.

The subjects of death and loss fill children's literature, possibly because we adults find the loss of a child so unthinkable. Perhaps equally painful is the loss of childhood itself, as evidenced by the excerpt above from Milne's *The House at Pooh Corner*. Here Christopher Robin and Pooh are saying goodbye forever due to the fact that Christopher Robin is going off to boarding school. Knowing this, what message do you think Christopher Robin is trying to convey to Pooh? What is Pooh's response? How do you think Milne wishes the reader to respond?

Using an Internet site such as YouTube or Jango, listen to the song by Loggins and Messina titled "House at Pooh Corner." What kind of emotion does the song evoke for you? Why do you think two adults would write and perform a song about a children's character?

Known as the Sage of Emporia, William Allen White owned and edited the Emporia Gazette. *He was one of the most famous journalists in America. White gained national prominence after the publication of his 1896 editorial "What's the Matter with Kansas?" He later became a leader of the Progressive movement and a political consultant for both President Theodore Roosevelt and President Franklin D. Roosevelt. Tragedy struck White and his family in 1921 with the sudden death of his sixteen-year-old daughter, Mary, from an accident.*

MARY WHITE

BY WILLIAM ALLEN WHITE

Emporia Gazette, May 17, 1921.

The *Associated Press* reports carrying the news of Mary White's death declared that it came as the result of a fall from a horse. How she would have hooted at that! She never fell from a horse in her life. Horses have fallen on her and with her—"I'm always trying to hold 'em in my lap," she used to say. But she was proud of few things, and one of them was that she could ride anything that had four legs and hair. Her death resulted not from a fall but from a blow on the head which fractured her skull, and the blow came from the limb of an overhanging tree on the parking.

The last hour of her life was typical of its happiness. She came home from a day's work at school, topped off by a hard grind with the copy on the High School Annual, and felt that a ride would refresh her. She climbed into her khakis, chattering to her mother about the work she was doing, and hurried to get her horse and be out on the dirt roads for the country air and the radiant green fields of spring. As she rode through the town on an easy gallop, she kept waving at passers-by. She knew everyone in town. For a decade the little figure in the long pigtail and the red hair ribbon has been familiar on the streets of Emporia, and she got in the way of speaking to those who nodded at her. She passed the Kerrs, walking the horse in front of the Normal Library, and waved at them; passed another friend a few hundred feet farther on, and waved at her.

The horse was walking, and as she turned into North Merchant Street she took off her cowboy hat, and the horse swung into a lope. She passed the Tripletts and waved her cowboy hat at them, still moving gayly north on Merchant Street. A Gazette carrier passed—a High School boy friend—and she waved at him, but with her bridle hand; the horse veered quickly, plunged into the parking where the low-hanging limb faced her and, while she still looked back waving, the blow came. But she did not fall from the horse; she slipped off, dazed a bit, staggered, and fell in a faint. She never quite recovered consciousness.

But she did not fall from the horse, neither was she riding fast. A year or so ago she used to go like the wind. But that habit was broken, and she used the horse to get into the open, to get fresh, hard exercise, and to work off a certain surplus energy that welled up in her and needed a physical outlet. The need has been in her heart for years. It was back of the impulse that kept the dauntless little brown-clad figure on the streets and country roads of the community and built into a strong, muscular body what had been a frail and sickly frame during the first years of her life. But the riding gave her more than a body. It released a gay and hardy soul. **She was the happiest thing in the world**. And she was happy because she was enlarging her horizon. She came to know all sorts and conditions of men; Charley O'Brien, the traffic cop, was one of her best friends. W. L. Holtz, the Latin teacher, was another. Tom O'Connor, farmer-politician, and the Rev. J. H. Rice, preacher and police judge, and Frank Beach, music master, were her special friends; and all the girls, black and white, above the track and below the track, in Pepville and Stringtown, were among her acquaintances. And she brought home riotous stories of her adventures. She loved to rollick; persiflage was her natural expression at home. Her humor was a continual bubble of joy. She seemed to think in hyperbole and metaphor. She was mischievous without malice, as full of faults as an old shoe. No angel was Mary White, but an easy girl to live with for she never nursed a grouch five minutes in her life.

With all her eagerness for the out-of-doors, she loved books. On her table when she left her room were a book by Conrad, one by Galsworthy, "Creative Chemistry" by E. E. Slosson, and a Kipling book. She read Mark Twain, Dickens, and Kipling before she was ten—all of their writings. Wells and Arnold Bennett particularly amused and diverted her. She was entered as a student in Wellesley for 1922; was assistant editor of the High School Annual this year, and in line for election to the editorship next year. She was a member of the executive committee of the High School Y.W.C.A.

Within the last two years she had begun to be moved by an **ambition to draw**. She began as most children do by scribbling in her school books, funny pictures. She bought cartoon magazines and took a course—rather casually, naturally, for she was, after all, a child with no strong purposes—and this year she tasted the first fruits of success by having her pictures accepted by the High School Annual. But the thrill of delight she got when Mr. Ecord, of the Normal Annual, asked her to do the cartooning for that book this spring, was too beautiful for words. She fell to her work with all her enthusiastic heart. Her drawings were accepted, and her pride—always repressed by a lively sense of the ridiculous figure she was cutting—was a really gorgeous thing to see. No successful artist every drank a deeper draft of satisfaction than she took from the little fame her work was getting among her schoolfellows. In her glory, she almost forgot her horse—but never her car.

For she used the car as a jitney bus. It was her social life. She never had a "party" in all her nearly seventeen years—wouldn't have one; but she never drove a block in her life that she didn't begin to fill the car with pick-ups! **Everybody rode with Mary White**—white and black, old and young, rich and poor, men and women. She liked nothing better than to fill the car with long-legged High School boys and an occasional girl, and parade the town. She never had a "date," nor went to a dance, except once with her brother Bill, and the "boy proposition" didn't interest her—yet. But young people—great spring-breaking, varnish-cracking, fender-bending, door-sagging carloads of "kids"—gave her great pleasure. Her zests were keen. But the most fun she ever had in her life was acting as chairman of the committee that got up the big turkey dinner for the poor folks at the county home; scores of pies, gallons of slaw, jam, cakes, preserves, oranges, and a wilderness of turkey were loaded into the car and taken to the county home. And, being of a practical turn of mind, she risked her own Christmas dinner to see that the poor folks actually got it all. Not that she was a cynic; she just disliked to tempt folks. While there, she found a blind colored uncle, very old, who could do nothing but make rag rugs, and she rustled up from her school friends rags enough to keep him busy for a season. The last engagement she tried to make was to take the guests at the county home out for a car ride. And the last endeavor of her life was to try to get a rest room for colored girls in the High School. She found one girl reading in the toilet, because there was no better place for a colored girl to loaf, and it inflamed her sense of injustice and she became a nagging harpy to those who she thought could remedy the evil. The poor she always had with her and was glad of it. She hungered and thirsted for righteousness; and was the most impious creature in the world. She joined the church without consulting her parents, not particularly for her soul's good. She never had a thrill of piety in her life, and would have hooted at a "testimony." But even as a little child, she felt the church was an agency for helping people to more of life's abundance, and she wanted to help. She never wanted help for herself. Clothes meant little to her. It was a fight to get a new rig on her; but eventually a harder fight to get it off. She never wore a jewel and had no ring but her High School class ring and never asked for anything but a wrist watch. She refused to have her hair up, though she was nearly seventeen. "Mother," she protested," you don't know how much I get by with, in my braided pigtails, that I could not with my hair up." Above every other passion of her life was her passion not to grow up, to be a child. The tomboy in her, which was big, seemed loath to be put away forever in skirts. She was a Peter Pan who refused to grow up.

Her funeral yesterday at the Congregational Church was as she would have wished it; no singing, no flowers except the big bunch of red roses from her brother Bill's Harvard classmen—heavens, how proud that would have made her!—and the red roses from the Gazette forces, in vases, at her head and feet. A short prayer: Paul's beautiful essay on "Love" from the Thirteenth Chapter of First Corinthians; some remarks about her democratic spirit by her friend, John H. J. Rice, pastor and police judge, which she would have deprecated if she could; a prayer sent down for her by her friend Carl Nau; and, opening the service, the slow, poignant movement from Beethoven's Moonlight Sonata, which she loved; and closing the service a cutting from the joyously melancholy first movement of Tchaikovsky's Pathetic Symphony, which she liked to hear, in certain moods, on the phonograph, then the Lord's Prayer by her friends in High School.

That was all.

For her pallbearers only her friends were chosen: her Latin teacher, W. L. Holtz; her High School principal, Rice Brown; her doctor, Frank Foncannon; her friend, W. W. Finney; her pal at the Gazette office, Walter Hughes; and her brother Bill. It would have made her smile to know that her friend, Charley

O'Brien, the traffic cop had been transferred from Sixth and Commercial to the corner near the church to direct her friends who came to bid her good-by.

A rift in the clouds in a gray day threw a shaft of sunlight upon her coffin as her nervous, energetic little body sank to its last sleep. But the soul of her, the glowing, gorgeous, fervent soul of her, surely was flaming in eager joy upon some other dawn.

Mary White was sixteen when she died from hitting her head on a low-hanging branch while riding. Such a tragedy would rock any family, but Mary's father was one of the most famous newspaper men in America. Often called the voice of Middle America, he was on intimate terms with the political leaders of his day, and was influential in national politics. His editorial eulogizing his daughter, "Mary White," became famous. What kind of person emerges from White's editorial? How would you characterize Mary White? What specific information does White provide to help readers "picture" his daughter, Mary?

Using the resources of your campus or local library, research the life of the typical American young woman of 1921. What would she have worn? What would she do for fun? How would she be expected to behave? What would her future most likely entail—college, marriage, or work? How does White's description of his daughter, Mary, compare to your findings?

DEATH

When a famous person dies, he or she is often remembered through an address, or eulogy, given by a close friend or family member. When Martin Luther King, Jr. was assassinated, Robert F. Kennedy gave a eulogy for him at his funeral, calling for the country to honor King's work by promoting peace in the nation. Brooke Shields, famous model and actress, spoke at Michael Jackson's funeral, where she painted a portrait of a loving friend, both funny and fragile—much different from popular views of Jackson. Such tributes are ways for the living to both honor and remember the dead. Following are three eulogies for three famous people given by equally famous individuals: actor Kevin Costner's eulogy for singer and actress Whitney Houston, former British Prime Minister Margaret Thatcher's eulogy for President Ronald Reagan, and media mogul Oprah Winfrey's eulogy for civil rights activist, Rosa Parks.

EULOGIES FOR WHITNEY HOUSTON, RONALD REAGAN, AND ROSA PARKS

By Kevin Costner, Margaret Thatcher, and Oprah Winfrey

EULOGY FOR WHITNEY HOUSTON BY KEVIN COSTNER

I'm going to say some stories. Maybe some of them you know, maybe some of them you don't. I wrote 'em down because I didn't want to miss anything.

The song "I Will Always Love You" almost wasn't. It wasn't supposed to be in the movie. The first choice was going to be "What Becomes of a Broken Heart." But it had been out the year before and in another movie, and we felt that it wouldn't have the impact and so we couldn't use it.

So what becomes of our broken hearts?

Whitney returns home today, to the place where it all began, and I urge us all, inside and outside, across the nation and around the world, to dry our tears, suspend our sorrow, and perhaps our anger, just long enough, just long enough to remember the sweet miracle of Whitney.

Never forgetting that Cissy and Bobbi Kristina sit among us. Your mother and I had a lot in common.

I know many at this moment are thinking, "Really?" [Laughter from the audience.] "She's a girl, you're a boy. You're white, she's black. We heard you like to sing. But our sister could really sing. So what am I talking about? Kevin Costner and Whitney Houston, they don't have anything in common at all." Well, you'd be wrong about that.

We both grew up in the Baptist church. It wasn't as big as this. My grandmother played the piano, and she led the choir and her two daughters, my mom and my aunt, both sang in it. . . .

I can see her in my own mind running around here as a skinny little girl, knowing everyone, everyone's business, knowing every inch of this place. I can also see her in trouble, too, trying to use that beautiful smile, trying to talk her way out of it, and Cissy not having any of it. . . .

At the height of her fame as a singer, I asked her to be my co-star in a movie called "The Bodyguard." I thought she was the perfect choice, but the red flags came out immediately. Maybe I should think this over a bit! [Laughs.]

I was reminded that this would be her first acting role. We could also think about another singer, was a suggestion. Maybe somebody white. Nobody ever said it out loud, but it was a fair question. It was. There would be a lot riding on this. Maybe a more experienced actress was the way to go. It was clear I really had to think about this.

I told everyone that I had taken notice that Whitney was black. The only problem was I thought she was perfect for what we were trying to do. . . .

The Whitney I knew, despite her success and worldwide fame, still wondered: Am I good enough? Am I pretty enough? Will they like me?

It was the burden that made her great and the part that made her stumble in the end.

Whitney, if you could hear me now I would tell you, you weren't just good enough—you were great. You sang the whole damn song without a band. You made the picture what it was.

A lot of leading men could have played my part, a lot of guys could have filled that role, but you, Whitney, I truly believe that you were the only one who could have played Rachel Marin at that time. [Applause.]

You weren't just pretty—you were as beautiful as a woman could be. And people didn't just like you, Whitney—they loved you.

I was your pretend bodyguard once not so long ago, and now you're gone, too soon, leaving us with memories of a little girl who stepped bravely in front of this church, in front of the ones that loved you first, in front of the ones that loved you best and loved you the longest.

Then, boldly, you stepped into the white-hot light of the world stage, and what you did is the rarest of achievements. You set the bar so high that professional singers, your own colleagues, they don't want to sing that little country song—what would be the point?

Now the only ones who sing your songs are young girls like you who are dreaming of being you some day.

And so to you, Bobbi Kristina, and to all those young girls who are dreaming that dream and maybe thinking they aren't good enough, I think Whitney would tell you: Guard your bodies, and guard the precious miracle of your own life, and then sing your hearts out—knowing that there's a lady in heaven who is making God Himself wonder how he created something so perfect.

So off you go, Whitney, off you go . . . escorted by an army of angels to your Heavenly Father. And when you sing before Him, don't you worry—you'll be good enough.

EULOGY FOR RONALD REAGAN BY MARGARET THATCHER
National Cathedral, Washington, D.C., June 11, 2004

We have lost a great president, a great American, and a great man, and I have lost a dear friend.

In his lifetime, Ronald Reagan was such a cheerful and invigorating presence that it was easy to forget what daunting historic tasks he set himself. He sought to mend America's wounded spirit, to restore the strength of the free world, and to free the slaves of communism. These were causes hard to accomplish and heavy with risk, yet they were pursued with almost a lightness of spirit, for Ronald Reagan also embodied another great cause—what Arnold Bennett once called "the great cause of cheering us all up." His policies had a freshness and optimism that won converts from every class and every nation, and ultimately, from the very heart of the "evil empire."

Yet his humour often had a purpose beyond humour. In the terrible hours after the attempt on his life, his easy jokes gave reassurance to an anxious world. They were evidence that in the aftermath of terror and in the midst of hysteria one great heart at least remained sane and jocular. They were truly grace under pressure. And perhaps they signified grace of a deeper kind. Ronnie himself certainly believed that he had been given back his life for a purpose. As he told a priest after his recovery "Whatever time I've got left now belongs to the big fella upstairs."

And surely, it is hard to deny that Ronald Reagan's life was providential when we look at what he achieved in the eight years that followed.

Others prophesied the decline of the West. He inspired America and its allies with renewed faith in their mission of freedom.

Others saw only limits to growth. He transformed a stagnant economy into an engine of opportunity.

Others hoped, at best, for an uneasy cohabitation with the Soviet Union. He won the Cold War, not only without firing a shot, but also by inviting enemies out of their fortress and turning them into friends.

I cannot imagine how any diplomat or any dramatist could improve on his words to Mikhail Gorbachev at the Geneva summit. "Let me tell you why it is we distrust you." Those words are candid and tough and they cannot have been easy to hear. But they are also a clear invitation to a new beginning and a new relationship that would be rooted in trust.

We live today in the world that Ronald Reagan began to reshape with those words. It is a very different world, with different challenges and new dangers. All in all, however, it is one of greater freedom and prosperity, one more hopeful than the world he inherited on becoming president.

As Prime Minister, I worked closely with Ronald Reagan for eight of the most important years of all our lives. We talked regularly, both before and after his presidency, and I have had time and cause to reflect on what made him a great president.

Ronald Reagan knew his own mind. He had firm principles and, I believe, right ones. He expounded them clearly. He acted upon them decisively.

When the world threw problems at the White House, he was not baffled or disorientated or overwhelmed.

He knew almost instinctively what to do.

When his aides were preparing option papers for his decision, they were able to cut out entire rafts of proposals that they knew "the old man" would never wear. When his allies came under Soviet or domestic pressure, they could look confidently to Washington for firm leadership, and when his enemies tested American resolve, they soon discovered that his resolve was firm and unyielding.

Yet his ideas, so clear, were never simplistic. He saw the many sides of truth. Yes, he warned that the Soviet Union had an insatiable drive for military power and territorial expansion, but he also sensed that it was being eaten away by systemic failures impossible to reform. Yes, he did not shrink from denouncing Moscow's "evil empire." But he realised that a man of good will might nonetheless emerge from within its dark corridors.

So the President resisted Soviet expansion and pressed down on Soviet weakness at every point until the day came when communism began to collapse beneath the combined weight of these pressures and its own failures. And when a man of good will did emerge from the ruins, President Reagan stepped forward to shake his hand and to offer sincere cooperation.

Nothing was more typical of Ronald Reagan than that large-hearted magnanimity, and nothing was more American.

Therein lies perhaps the final explanation of his achievements. Ronald Reagan carried the American people with him in his great endeavours because there was perfect sympathy between them. He and they loved America and what it stands for: freedom and opportunity for ordinary people.

As an actor in Hollywood's golden age, he helped to make the American dream live for millions all over the globe. His own life was a fulfilment of that dream. He never succumbed to the embarrassment some people feel about an honest expression of love of country. He was able to say "God bless America" with equal fervour in public and in private. And so he was able to call confidently upon his fellow countrymen to make sacrifices for America and to make sacrifices for those who looked to America for hope and rescue.

With the lever of American patriotism, he lifted up the world. And so today, the world in Prague, in Budapest, in Warsaw, in Sofia, in Bucharest, in Kiev and in Moscow itself—the world mourns the passing of the great liberator and echoes his prayer God bless America.

Ronald Reagan's life was rich not only in public achievement, but also in private happiness. Indeed, his public achievements were rooted in his private happiness.

The great turning point of his life was his meeting and marriage with Nancy. On that, we have the plain testimony of a loving and grateful husband. "Nancy came along and saved my soul."

We share her grief today, but we also share her pride and the grief and pride of Ronnie's children. For the final years of his life, Ronnie's mind was clouded by illness. That cloud has now lifted. He is himself again, more himself than at any time on this earth, for we may be sure that the Big fellow upstairs never forgets those who remember Him. And as the last journey of this faithful pilgrim took him beyond the sunset, and as heaven's morning broke, I like to think, in the words of Bunyan, that "all the trumpets sounded on the other side."

We here still move in twilight, but we have one beacon to guide us that Ronald Reagan never had. We have his example. Let us give thanks today for a life that achieved so much for all of God's children.

EULOGY FOR ROSA PARKS BY OPRAH WINFREY

"...God uses good people to do great things."

Reverend Braxton, family, friends, admirers, and this amazing choir:

I—I feel it an honor to be here to come and say a final goodbye.

I grew up in the South, and Rosa Parks was a hero to me long before I recognized and understood the power and impact that her life embodied. I remember my father telling me about this colored woman who had refused to give up her seat. And in my child's mind, I thought, "She must be really big." I thought she must be at least a hundred feet tall. I imagined her being stalwart and strong and carrying a shield to hold back the white folks.

And then I grew up and had the esteemed honor of meeting her. And wasn't that a surprise. Here was this petite, almost delicate lady who was the personification of grace and goodness. And I thanked her then. I said, "Thank you," for myself and for every colored girl, every colored boy, who didn't have heroes who were celebrated.

I thanked her then.

And after our first meeting I realized that God uses good people to do great things. And I'm here today to say a final thank you, Sister Rosa, for being a great woman who used your life to serve, to serve us all. That day that you refused to give up your seat on the bus, you, Sister Rosa, changed the trajectory of my life and the lives of so many other people in the world. I would not be standing here today nor standing where I stand every day had she not chosen to sit down. I know that. I know that. I know that. I know that, and I honor that. Had she not chosen to say we shall not—we shall not be moved.

So I thank you again, Sister Rosa, for not only confronting the one white man who[se] seat you took, not only confronting the bus driver, not only for confronting the law, but for confronting history, a history that for 400 years said that you were not even worthy of a glance, certainly no consideration. I thank you for not moving.

And in that moment when you resolved to stay in that seat, you reclaimed your humanity and you gave us all back a piece of our own. I thank you for that. I thank you for acting without concern. I often thought about what that took, knowing the climate of the times and what could have happened to you, what it took to stay seated. You acted without concern for yourself and made life better for us all. We shall not be moved.

I marvel at your will.

I celebrate your strength to this day.

And I am forever grateful, Sister Rosa, for your courage, your conviction.

I owe you—to succeed.

I will not be moved.

Choose from one of the eulogies that you just read and answer the following questions:

1. What personal details or stories, if any, did the author provide about the deceased?

2. What value did the deceased hold for his or her community?

3. How did the author view the deceased?

Imagine your own death, far into the future, from natural causes. How would you want to be remembered? What accomplishments would you like to be known for, both professionally and personally? In a short essay (2 to 3 paragraphs) write a eulogy for yourself.

MAJOR ASSIGNMENTS

MAJOR WRITING ASSIGNMENT # 1:
WRITING A MEMOIR ABOUT DEATH

BACKGROUND

Writing about death, or any of life's experiences, allows us to examine our feelings and beliefs through the filter of memory. A memoir functions as a kind of synthesis, allowing the author to see the experience within the context of his or her life as a whole, often bringing hidden meaning to light. A father writes about the death of his teenaged daughter and learns to celebrate her wild, untamed spirit; a man writes about coming to terms with his own mortality and discovers comfort in the knowledge that he is a part of the chain of life; a scholar dying of cancer gains strength from writing a scathing denunciation of the medical profession she hopes will nonetheless save her life. Memoir writing is as valuable to the author as it is to the reader in that both learn from the process of writing about real, lived experience.

A number of authors in this book write about their own personal experiences with death, from Anna Belle Kaufman and William Allen White—who both write about the loss of a child—to Mitch Albom, who writes about the loss of a beloved professor. What personal experiences have you had with death? How did they affect you? What did you learn from the experience?

ASSIGNMENT

Read, or refresh your memory of, a few of the works by Mitch Albom, Anna Belle Kaufman, E. B. White, Audre Lorde, and William Allen White. Using these pieces as models and inspiration, write a memoir essay that uses dialogue, dramatic pacing, and descriptive language to convey a specific experience you have had with death. While the topic of your memoir does not have to be about the death of someone you knew, it does have to be about your personal reaction to some aspect of death.

QUESTIONS FOR INVENTION

1. Have you ever lost someone in your family to death, such as a parent, grandparent, sibling, spouse, or child? If so, what was your experience with losing this person, beyond the inevitable grief?

2. Have you ever lost someone close to you, like a friend, teacher, or co-worker? If so, how did their death affect you?

3. Today's technology allows us to see and hear events from around the world almost as fast as they occur—often in graphic detail. Have you ever seen or read about deaths in the media that affected you strongly, such as the tragic deaths at the Aurora, Colorado movie theater, the attack on the World Trade Center, or the wreck of the Costa cruise ship off the coast of Italy? If so, how did you react?

ABOUT MEMOIR ESSAYS

As you begin to draft your experience with death, keep in mind that a memoir should:

- focus on one specific incidence or memory;
- use vivid, specific language that describes and recreates scenes, people, and meaningful dialogue;
- provide an indication as to why this memory is significant to you.

MAJOR WRITING ASSIGNMENT # 2:
TAKING A STAND REGARDING DEATH

BACKGROUND

Catholic nun, Helen Prejean, writes persuasively against the death penalty, while Jessica Mitford critiques the funeral industry, and Jenna Worthham wonders how social media sites like Facebook should handle the death of its users. Death, as a topic, covers a number of controversial issues, from important social questions such as euthanasia, to local issues such as whether or not a community needs another cemetery.

ASSIGNMENT

Using a topic of your choice, take a position in regard to your subject. For example, you may agree with Helen Prejean that the death penalty should be abolished, or with Jessica Mitford that funerals are too costly and elaborate. Whatever your topic and views, write a persuasive essay with a clear position, good reasons, convincing evidence, and attention to audience. You may wish to do some research using the resources of your campus library and/or the Internet to find other opinions on the subject, as well as evidence to support your position. Remember, whatever topic you choose, your goal is not so much to change the views of your audience as it is to construct an argument your audience will give serious consideration.

QUESTIONS FOR RESEARCH AND INVENTION

1. What makes your topic controversial?

2. What possible stands can you take in regard to your topic?

3. For what major reasons would people agree with your position? Disagree?

4. What audience are you identifying for your essay? Your class, your local community, or just a general audience?

5. Where might you find other essays, newspaper articles, Web sites, blogs, or books on your topic?

ABOUT PERSUASIVE ESSAYS

As you begin to draft your essay, keep in mind that all persuasive essays share the same basic features:

- a clearly stated position in regard to your topic;

- good reasons that support your position;

- convincing evidence to support your reasons;

- a careful consideration of your audience through counterarguments raised and refuted.

MAJOR WRITING ASSIGNMENT # 3:
ANALYZING THE RHETORIC OF SYMPATHY CARDS

BACKGROUND

Death is an unfortunate fact of life, and most people respond when hearing of a death with expressions of care and concern, often in the form of a greeting card expressing sympathy for the person's loss. Like an advertisement, a painting, or a music video, sympathy cards are texts whose meaning lies not only in the actual words they contain, but in the images (and in the case of e-cards, music) they depict. Implicit arguments exist in all of these media forms, yet we often allow the images, designs, colors, and sounds to impress upon us without much thought as to why or how these effects are achieved. A rhetorical analysis of sympathy cards can tell us a great deal about how our culture views death, grief, and loss.

ASSIGNMENT

Using Google, Bing, or another Internet search engine, examine the print and e-cards available on a number of greeting card companies' Web sites, such as http://www.americangreetings.com; http://www.bluemountain.com; or http://www.hallmark.com. Using specific examples from these Web sites, from a retail outlet, or from your own collection, write a rhetorical analysis of a sympathy greeting card or a group of cards. Be sure to include specific design elements to support your analysis.

QUESTIONS FOR INVENTION

1. Who is the intended audience for the card or cards you analyzed?

2. What message does the card or cards literally provide in words?

3. What meaning is created by the images? By the music?

4. What effect do the design elements and compositional features (font, layout, use of space, color, graphics, etc.) convey?

ABOUT A RHETORICAL ANALYSIS

As you begin your analysis of your chosen sympathy card or cards, keep in mind that such an analysis should include:

- a brief description of the sympathy card or cards;
- a clear statement of the intended effect the card has on the recipient;
- the audience for whom the card is intended;
- an analysis of the design elements and compositional features of the card or cards;
- specific evidence from the card or cards to support the analysis;
- a color copy of the card or cards attached to the final draft of the assignment.

MAJOR WRITING ASSIGNMENT # 4:
WRITING A EULOGY FOR SOMEONE YOU KNOW OR ADMIRE

BACKGROUND

A eulogy is a written or oral speech given at a funeral or at a memorial service for someone who has died. The practice began with the ancient Greeks, from whom we get the word "eulogy," meaning "good words."

Eulogies are often given by a family member or close friend of the deceased, a member of the clergy, or a prominent member of the community. The point of this practice is to show respect and honor to the dead person, to say farewell, as well as to celebrate their life and accomplishments. A eulogy often provides as much comfort to the living as it honors the deceased.

ASSIGNMENT

Review William Allen White's editorial on the death of his daughter, Kevin Costner's eulogy for Whitney Houston, Oprah Winfrey's eulogy for Rosa Parks, as well as Margaret Thatcher's eulogy for Ronald Reagan. How do you feel about these people after reading these tributes? How do you think the authors felt about them? Using the resources of your campus library and /or the Internet, you may want to research other famous eulogies or read samples of eulogies written by ordinary people about their friends and family who have passed away. You can choose to write a eulogy for someone who has already died, or for someone who is still alive. You can also choose a friend or family member to honor, or select someone you admire who is famous.

Regardless of your choice, write a eulogy that provides a clear picture of the person, including biographical facts such as his or her family background, education, profession, spouse, children, and accomplishments. Be sure to include how you felt about this person.

QUESTIONS FOR RESEARCH AND INVENTION

1. Where and when was the deceased born?

2. Who were his or her parents? Brothers and sisters?

3. What schools did he or she attend? Any degrees earned?

4. What job or profession did he or she perform?

5. Any war or military service?

6. Any noteworthy accomplishments?

7. Any church affiliation?

8. Marriage or children?

9. Any hobbies or sports?

10. Any good friends or membership in service clubs?

11. Any special stories or anecdotes he or she told or were told about them?

12. What do close friends and family members say about him or her?

ABOUT EULOGIES

As you begin to write about the person you have chosen to eulogize, keep in mind what goes into a good eulogy:

- a clear sense of how you respect and value this person;

- biographical details that provide information about the person's family, background, education, profession, and accomplishments;

- personal details or stories that help paint a picture of what this person was like;

- words that express his or her value and loss to the community.

MAJOR WRITING ASSIGNMENT #5:
RESEARCHING A TOPIC ON DEATH AND DYING

BACKGROUND

A look through the Table of Contents of this book alone shows just how many topics exist relating to death and dying. What interests you about death? This assignment allows you to explore any aspect of the subject that you desire through research. Perhaps you have always been interested in the Mexican practice of visiting one's dead relatives on one day each year on the *Día de los Muertos*, or Day of the Dead. Or maybe you'd like to know more about the ancient Celtic festival of the dead, *Samhain*. Some people have always wondered about whether or not there is life after death, while others are fascinated with how death is depicted in painting or in poetry. Whatever topic you choose, this assignment allows you to explore the topic in depth as you practice writing to inform others.

ASSIGNMENT

One you have chosen your topic, use the resources of your campus library and the Internet to find sources relating to your subject. Make sure your search includes a variety of sources, such as Web sites, books, journal articles, newspaper articles, and personal interviews. Don't be afraid to ask your campus or local reference librarians for help finding sources. Once you have gathered and read your material, write a research paper that clearly states your take on the subject, including a summary of the information you found, organized in an interesting and easy-to-follow manner. Be sure to attribute the work of others in your paper by using a style of documentation, such as MLA.

QUESTIONS FOR RESEARCH AND INVENTION

1. How did humans bury their dead in prehistoric times?

2. How does one prepare for one's own death or the death of a loved one?

3. What are the psychological stages of grief?

4. How does one learn to become a mortician or a funeral director?

5. How do other cultures deal with death and dying?

6. How has death and dying been depicted in art? In literature? In film?

7. What medical advancements have been made in the treatment of the dying?

8. What is the actual physical process the body experiences as it dies?

9. Is there life after death? Can we communicate with the dead?

10. What mythological creatures are associated with death and dying?

ABOUT RESEARCH ASSIGNMENTS

As you begin your research topic, recognize that good research papers should have:

- a clearly stated thesis;
- information from a variety of authoritative sources;
- skillful synthesis and interpretation of information;
- an effective and clear organization;
- smoothly integrated quoted or paraphrased material using a style of documentation, such as MLA, or APA.

FILMOGRAPHY

DOCUMENTARIES

The Emotional Life. Documentary. PBS, ongoing series, premiered January 2010. Episode titled: "Grief and Loss".

A Family Undertaking. Documentary. PBS, 2004.

Flight from Death: The Quest for Immortality. Documentary. The Orchard Studio, 2005.

On Our Own Terms: Moyer on Dying in America. Documentary. PBS, 2005.

Secrets of the Dead: Crime Scene Investigations Meet History. PBS series, including episodes titled, "Mystery of the Black Death," and "Murder at Stonehenge."

FEATURE FILMS

Bucket List. Film. Warner Brothers, 2007. Director, Rob Reiner.

Dead Man Walking. Film. 1995, Director, Tim Robbins.

Death Takes a Holiday. Film. Paramount Studios. 1934. Director, Mitchell Leisen.

Love Story. Film. Paramount Pictures, 1970. Director, Arthur Hiller.

Our Town. Film. Paramount Studios, 1940. Director, Sam Wood.

Wit. Film. HBO, 2001. Director, Mike Nichols (based on a play by Margaret Edison)

TELEVISION SERIES

Dead Like Me. TV Series, MGM, 2003-2004.
Six Feet Under. TV Series, HBO, 2001-2005.

WEBSITES

Encyclopedia of Death and Dying. www.deathreference.com

Greeting Card Association. www.greetingcard.org

The Postcard Museum. www.emotionscards.com/museumn

Life Gem created diamonds. www.lifegem.com

"Of Death" by Francis Bacon (public domain) www.authorrama.com

"Should the death penalty be banned as a form of punishment?
     BalancedPolitics.org/death_penalty.htm

"Death and Dying: Some News is so Big it Needs its Own Page." *The Huffington
     Post.* www.huffingtonpost.com/news/death--dying.

"So You Want to Get a PhD in the Humanities?" See youtube.com. and
     Xtranormal.com.

WORKS CITED

Albom, Mitch. *Tuesdays with Morrie: An Old Man, a Young Man, and Life's Greatest Lesson*. New York: Broadway Books, 2007, 24–38. Print.

Blue Öyster Cult. "(Don't Fear) the Reaper." *Agents of Fortune*. Columbia, 1976. CD.

Cullen, Lisa Takeuchi. "Ashes to Ashes, Dust to Diamonds: How to Turn Your Loved One into Jewelry, and Why," in *Remember Me: A Lively Tour of the New American Way of Death*. New York: HarperCollins, 2006, 61–75. Print.

Costner, Kevin. Eulogy for Whitney Houston. New Hope Baptist Church, Newark, New Jersey. 18 Feb. 2012. Web. 28 Feb. 2012.

Dillard, Annie. "Death of a Moth." *Harpers Magazine*, May 1976. 26–27. Print.

Hudson, Ryan. "Note to Self: You Can't Cheat Death." Cartoon. *Channelate. com*. 22 May 2008. Web. 21 Oct. 2010.

Jars of Clay. "All My Tears." *Good Monsters*. Essential, 2006. CD.

Jones, Constance. *R.I.P.: The Complete Book of Death and Dying*. New York: Sonesong Press/HarperCollins, 1997, 44–47. Print.

Jokinen, Tom. "Love Your Hair, Who's Your Embalmer?" *Curtains: Adventures of an Undertaker-in-Training.* Cambridge, MA: Perseus, 2010. 49–58. Print.

Lambrecht, Claire. "The Truth About Grief: What's Wrong with a Nation of Mourners?" *Salon.com.* Salon Media Group, 12 Feb. 2011. Web. 20 Feb. 2011.

Kaufman, Anna Belle. "Things That Went Bump in the Night: A Grieving Mother Hangs on for a Haunting." *Utne Reader,* Jan.–Feb. 2011. 31–35. Print.

Kübler-Ross, Elisabeth. "On the Fear of Death." *On Death and Dying.* New York: Macmillan, 1969, 1–9. Print.

Lorde, Audre. "The Transformation of Silence into Language and Action," *The Cancer Journals: Special Edition.* San Francisco: Aunt Lute Books, 1997. 16–22. Print.

Milne, A. A. *The House at Pooh Corner.* New York: Dutton Juvenile, 1988. Print.

Mitford, Jessica. "The American Way of Death." *The American Way of Death, Revisited.* New York: Knopf, 1998, 14–19. Print.

Moore, Jessica. "Death is Only a Horizon." *Open.Salon.com.* Salon Media Group, 13 Feb. 2012. Web. 14 Feb. 2012.

Murray, Sarah. "When Morning Goes Viral: The 2.5 Million Tweets After Steve Jobs' Death Prove Just How Profoundly Social Media Have Transformed Mourning." *Salon.com.* Salon Media Group, 7 October 2011. Web. 14 Feb. 2012.

Nordland, Rod. "How Grim is My Valley: An Epidemic of Young Suicides Sweeps an Old Welsh Coal Area, Linked Only by a Social-Networking Web Site." *Newsweek,* March 2008. *Lexis-Nexis.* Web. 14 Feb. 2012.

Prejean, Helen, C.S.J. *Dead Man Walking*: *An Eyewitness Account of the Death Penalty in the United States*. New York: Random House, 1993, 86–95. Print.

Roach, Mary. "Life after Death: Of Human Decay and What Can Be Done about It." *Stiff: The Curious Lives of Human Cadavers*. New York: Norton, 2003. 61–72. Print.

Sims, Michael. "All the Dead are Vampires: A Natural-Historical Look at Our Love-Hate Relationship with Dead People." *The Chronicle Review of Higher Education*, June 2010. Print.

Sipress, David. "This City is Becoming Unliveable." Cartoon. *The New Yorker*. Sep. 2010: 56. Print.

Stanley, Ralph. "O Death." *O Brother, Where Art Thou?* Lost Highway, 2000. CD.

Tecumseh, Chief of the Shawnee. "Attitude Toward Death." *Poems and Readings for Funerals and Memorials*, Luisa Moncada, ed. London: New Holland, 2009. 152. Print.

Thatcher, Margaret. "Eulogy to the Great Liberator." National Cathedral, Washington, D.C. 11 June 2004. Web. 28 Feb. 2012.

Thomas, Lewis. "On Natural Death." *The Medusa and the Snail: More Notes of a Biology Watcher*. New York: Bantam, 1980. 83–86. Print.

Trebay, Guy. "Lost to AIDS, but Still Friended." *New York Times*, 13 Dec. 2009. Web. 14 Feb. 2012.

Winfrey, Oprah. ". . . God Uses Good People to Do Great Things." Metropolitan AME Church, Washington, D.C. 31 October 2005. Web. 28 Feb. 2012.

White, E. B. "Once More to the Lake," in *Essays of E. B. White*. New York: McGraw-Hill College, 2000, 246–256. Print.

White, William Allen. "Mary White" Editorial. *Emporia Gazette*. 17 May 1921. Web. 8 August 2011.

Wilson, Rainn, et al. "What Do You Hope Happens When You Die?" *Soulpancake: Chew on Life's Big Questions.* New York: Hyperion, 2010. 190-91. Print.

Woolf, Virginia. "The Death of the Moth," in *The Death of the Moth and Other Essays.* San Diego: Harcourt, 1974. 3–6. Print.

Wortham, Jenna. "As Facebook Users Die, Ghosts Reach Out," *New York Times,* 17 July 2010. Web. 22 June 2012.

NOTES

NOTES